INTRODUCTION TO TECHNICAL ANALYSIS

Monika Lee
107 Legacy Lane
Durham, NC 27713

Also by Martin J. Pring

Martin Pring on Market Momentum

Technical Analysis Explained: The Successful Investor's Guide to Spotting
Investment Trends and Turning Points

INTRODUCTION TO TECHNICAL ANALYSIS

MARTIN J. PRING
Publisher, *The Intermarket Review*

McGraw-Hill
New York   San Francisco   Washington, D.C.   Auckland   Bogotá
Caracas   Lisbon   London   Madrid   Mexico City   Milan
Montreal   New Delhi   San Juan   Singapore
Sydney   Tokyo   Toronto

Library of Congress Cataloging-in-Publication Data

Pring, Martin J.
    Martin Pring's introduction to technical analysis / Martin
J. Pring.
        p.   cm.
    Includes index.
    ISBN 0-07-032933-8
    1. Investment analysis. I. Title.
HG4529.P748   1997
332.6—dc21   97-9028
                                                           CIP

McGraw-Hill

A Division of The **McGraw·Hill** Companies

P/N 913621-4
PART OF
ISBN 0-07-032933-8

*The sponsoring editor for this book was Allyson Arias, the editing
supervisor was Caroline R. Levine, and the production supervisor was
Clare B. Stanley. This book was set in Fairfield by Donald A. Feldman
of McGraw-Hill's Professional Book Group composition unit.*

Printed and bound by R. R. Donnelley & Sons Company.

McGraw-Hill books are available at special quantity discounts to use
as premiums and sales promotions, or for use in corporate training
programs. For more information, please write to the Director of
Special Sales, McGraw-Hill, 11 West 19th Street, New York, NY
10011. Or contact your local bookstore.

 This book is printed on recycled, acid-free paper containing a
minimum of 50% recycled, de-inked fiber.

To my daughter, Connie

CONTENTS

PREFACE

This preface is not the preface for the *workbook* you are reading, but rather, it is designed for the CD which accompanies it. In truth, the *workbook* accompanies the CD—providing an easy reference source for all the charts and commentary it contains. The menus on the CD are user friendly and the comprehensive index makes locating topics a snap!

The CD tutorial concept for teaching technical analysis began forming in my mind several years ago. There is a substantial amount of written material on the many aspects of this fascinating subject, but I found very little giving the beginning technician a comprehensive overview of the basic principles. Even my own book, *Technical Analysis Explained*, assumes the reader is a beginner with little or no knowledge of technical analysis. It covers the basic principles quickly and moves on to describe a substantial number of intermediate and advanced principles. My thoughts were "this could be intimidating for anyone who really needs to start at square one and build on their knowledge." If this is how you feel, this CD and accompanying workbook were designed for you. Think of them as the primer to *Technical Analysis Explained*. And because technical analysis deals with charts, what better way to demonstrate how charts are interpreted and how to apply the tools of the technician than to use the multimedia, interactive environment of a CD?

You will find both the CD and workbook broken down into 13 chapters, each covering a specific aspect of technical analysis. Every chapter has three elements, each building on the last. The first element of the CD is a series of animated presentations explaining the concepts behind the principles covered in the chapter. The second element is one or more movies demonstrating, with actual market examples, how these principles should be applied. The movies provide a good technician's view of what you will see and be applying when you're ready to begin charting on your own. And lastly, there is an interactive quiz which will test your newly acquired knowledge of the current chapter using a multiple choice format. The test can be taken as many times as you wish and is automatically scored, so you can compare your results to the last two tests you took and see your improvement!

Because my philosophy is to keep things as simple as possible (although life rarely is), you will find that I don't apply any fluff and tell it like it is. In learning the art of technical analysis, the first and most important lesson you need to learn is that technical analysis has both strength and weaknesses. If you are looking for the perfect indicator, or the path to instant profits, this is not the course for you (and I don't believe, if the truth were told, that such a course does, or ever will, exist). In this spirit, I am reminded of a comment someone recently made to me: "The holy grail is knowing that there is no holy grail." I think they hit the nail on the head.

Good luck and good charting!

Please use the information below for question 1.

Martin J. Pring
President
International Institute for Economic Research, Inc.
Sarasota, FL 34239
Publishers of The Intermarket Review

ACKNOWLEDGMENTS

The preparation of this Tutorial CD and workbook has taken a considerable amount of time and effort. Special thanks go to Jimmie Sigsway WGM (World's Greatest Mother-in-law) for dutifully proof reading the manuscript and CD text. Also to Connie Pring for helping out with her brother and in the office so her parents could work.

The CD would not have been possible without the talents of Jeff Howard, our multimedia programming consultant, who, as usual, constantly bent over backwards to meet our demanding deadlines and answer the Great Question: "Hey Jeff, can we do this?"

Special thanks also go to David Conti and Phil Ruppel at McGraw-Hill for their encouragement and support in publishing this unique concept.

Above all, my deepest debt goes to my wife Lisa who has spent countless hours creating the animated presentations that form the bulk of the tutorial, while simultaneously developing a web page (www.pring.com) and publishing our monthly newsletter, *The Intermarket Review*. Whenever I see those flashing arrows and animated text I am constantly reminded of the long, lonely hours spent on this huge project.

PART ONE

BASIC CONCEPTS

We will begin by taking a look at some of the principal building blocks of technical analysis. Everyone has different trading or investment objectives: some short-term, others long-term; some conservative, others speculative. May I say at the outset, it doesn't matter what time frame you work in—daily, yearly, or more. The principles of technical analysis are the same. Most of the examples will use daily charts, but the basic principles can be applied to long-term trends and vice versa. The more I work with markets, the more I appreciate the fact that *prices are determined by changes in mass psychology*, and psychology is just as relevant in short-term charts as it is in longer-term ones. It's also just as relevant over different markets around the globe. It doesn't matter whether you are in New York looking at a chart of Microsoft or in Malaysia following tin futures. Markets reflect human action, and people tend to make the same mistakes. Human nature is more or less constant. Fortunately, these constant emotional swings keep reappearing in the charts.

BASIC PRINCIPLES

SOME GROUND RULES

In a good novel, the author often grabs the attention of readers with some pretty exciting stuff right at the beginning. We are going to start with the "dry" material and then work into the more interesting stuff. First some basic pointers.

1. The term *securities* refers to all freely traded markets. In this book, stocks, bonds, commodities, currencies, or any other freely traded entity will be designated as securities. The generic term makes the discussion less cumbersome and indicates that the principles can be applied to all freely traded markets.

2. I will demonstrate many of the principles of technical analysis, but I want you to be aware that this art is not perfect. It can and does fail from time to time. *In technical analysis we are dealing in probabilities,* and even when the odds are heavily in our favor it's still possible that things won't work out as we would like or expect.

3. With the advent of computers and computerized trading, it is now possible to come up with some pretty sophisticated indicators and methods. *Don't use complexity as a crutch. Keep things as simple as possible.* My experience is that people often use complexity as a substitute for not thinking. For this reason, it's of paramount importance to stick with simplicity, and I've tried to do that in this text.

4. Technical analysis can do a lot for you if you have the patience, discipline, and objectivity to apply the basic principles. But I warn you: *It is no sure-fire system.* Indeed,

there is none as far as the markets are concerned. Commercials you see promising consistent, easy, or fast profits are false. Believe me, if the advertisers had found the "system," they would be quietly collecting millions in the marketplace, not risking their time and money in promoting their ideas.

WHAT IS TECHNICAL ANALYSIS?

Now that we have covered the preliminaries, we can begin to discuss technical analysis. In a sense, the word *technical* is a bit misleading, since we are really concerned with studying various forms of pricing information as displayed on graphs.

Prices are determined by the expectations of those already in the market and those contemplating getting in. The price of a specific security at any one time is determined by the knowledge, hopes, fears, and expectations of all those people who already own it or who might be thinking about owning it. If I am sitting with cash, I am affecting the price just as much as anyone who has bought the security—for by holding back from making a purchase, I am keeping the price lower than it otherwise would be. It's the attitude of people that is important. Garfield Drew, a well-thought-of technician earlier in this century, once said in referring to the price of stocks, "They never sell for what they are worth but for what people *think* they are worth." This statement applies to any traded security. It is important to understand that market participants look ahead, anticipate future developments, and take action now.

If you are on the railroad tracks and see a train coming, is it likely that you will wait until the last moment before getting off the tracks? No. You anticipate that the train is going to run you over and you get off the tracks right away. Market participants are the same. The difference is that not all participants get the news at the same time. Some get the news from a different angle, and different people have different attitudes toward the same anticipated developments. For example, if you are an investor and anticipate that some forthcoming bad news will create a short-term reaction in an ongoing bull market, you probably won't take any action. On the other hand, if you are a highly leveraged short-term trader, you would be foolish not to sell. Otherwise you would stand to lose all your profit. The same news, then, can affect different people in different ways. The sum of the attitude of all participants, and potential participants, is reflected in one thing and one thing only—the price. This discounting mechanism is the reason that markets bottom when the news is bad and peak when it is good. At such points of extreme emotional activity, participants have already factored today's headlines into the price and begun to anticipate tomorrow's headlines.

This is all well and good. But it would be of little use except for the fact that prices move in trends, and once a trend begins it tends to perpetuate. The art of technical analysis, then, is to try to identify trend changes at an early stage and maintain an investment or trading posture until the weight of the evidence shows or proves that the trend has reversed. I'll repeat that very important statement: *The art of technical analysis is to try to identify trend changes at an early stage and maintain an investment or trading posture until the weight of the evidence shows or proves that the trend has reversed.* In technical analysis, the "evidence" is provided by the numerous indicators and principles that we shall learn about in the course of this book. They include price patterns, trendlines, moving averages, momentum, and so forth.

One principle that emerges from this definition of technical analysis is that once a new trend emerges, it should be assumed that it is still in force until enough indicators have given reversal signals. Always assume the prevailing trend is intact until proved otherwise. Technical analysis does not promise that you can identify the top or the bottom, merely the area of a top and the area of a bottom.

Since trends tend to perpetuate, it's still possible to do quite well in most situations. However, it's best to remember that technical analysis is far from perfect, even when correctly interpreted. It can certainly help in identifying the direction of a trend, but there is no known method of consistently forecasting its magnitude.

METHODS OF PLOTTING CHARTS

Over the years, technicians have devised a number of different ways of physically representing market data on charts. In this text it is not feasible to consider them all. However, we will look at the most popular—a bar chart, a close-only (or line) chart, a point-and-figure chart, and finally, a candlestick chart.

BAR CHART

Most charting methods plot the price on the vertical, or Y, axis and the time on the horizontal, or X, axis. This is certainly true of the most widely used form of charting—namely, the bar chart (Chart 1-1), in which the portrayal of prices is achieved with vertical bars. The bars themselves usually have at least one horizontal tick mark. The bar represents the trading range for the period in question. The top of the bar records the high and the bottom records the low. A tick mark to the left represents the opening price, and a tick mark to the

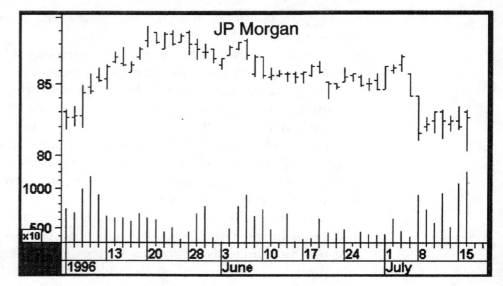

CHART 1-1. *J. P. Morgan.*

right indicates the closing, or settlement, price. The bars also reflect the time period in question. If the data is weekly, the bar will reflect the Monday opening, the Friday close, and the intraday high and low for the week. In daily charts the bars reflect the daily trading range; and so forth. The advantage of bar charts is that they visually provide a lot of information. The most important parts of a bar chart are the opening and closing prices. The opening is helpful because it reflects the psychology of market participants as they begin the trading session. Closing prices are important because they reflect traders and investors who are willing to take home a position overnight. As we will see in Chapter Six, sometimes the characteristics of a single bar can provide clues as to future market action.

Underneath most charts you will see more vertical bars. These measure trading activity, or volume, for the particular time period in question. Most of the indicators and techniques used in technical analysis represent a statistical variation on the price, so it is extremely useful to monitor volume—because it reflects a different variable, one that is independent of price.

LINE CHART

In the line or close-only style of charting (Chart 1-2), the highs, openings, and lows are ignored. Only the closing prices are considered. The continuous line joins the closing prices. The line chart does not provide as much visual information as the bar chart, but in many respects it is more useful. First, since the high and low are ignored, much of the random noise that occurs during the trading session is eliminated. Second, because of the cleaner chart look, it is much easier to visually spot the prevailing trend; this means that reversals are also easier to identify. Third, the closing price is important, since it reflects only those participants who are prepared to hold the security overnight or over a weekend. These are the people who have a greater conviction and are more likely to be in tune with the prevailing psychological trend. Finally, close-

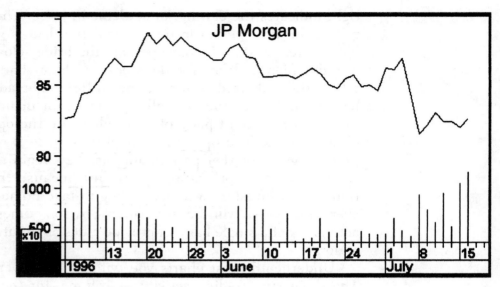

CHART 1-2. *J. P. Morgan.*

only charts can be plotted for longer time spans, since bar charts require a space between the bars, and too many periods will visually clutter up the chart.

POINT-AND-FIGURE CHART

The point-and-figure charting method (Chart 1-3) differs from all the others in that the horizontal axis does not measure time, but rather the amount of trading within a given price range. The point-and-figure chart consists of a series of 0's and X's, known as *boxes.* The 0's reflect declining prices and the X's, rising prices. Each box is set for a certain price movement. For example, it is normal in stock market charting to set each box to $1 for stocks trading above $20. Thus every time the price moves up by $1, a new, higher X is drawn on the chart. If it moves up by 99 cents, no new box appears. However, if the price declines by $1—that is, $1.99 from the high—then a 0 is plotted.

Since price fluctuations for any given security are largely a function of time, long-term charts are constructed with large boxes and short-term ones with smaller boxes. The point-and-

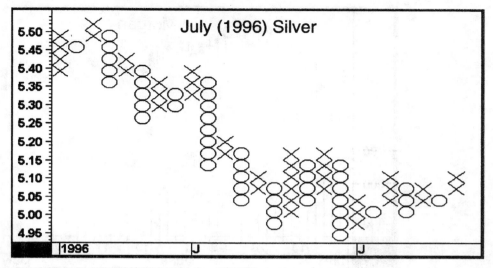

CHART 1-3. *July (1966) silver.*

figure chart takes a bit of getting used to, but its proponents are adamant that it is a very valuable form of charting.

CANDLESTICK CHART

The candlestick form of charting (Chart 1-4) has gained in popularity in the last few years. This method originated in Japan several centuries ago and basically offers the same information as bar charts. The difference is that candlestick charts can often make it easier to spot certain technical phenomena not readily apparent with a quick glance at a bar chart.

The candles consist of a vertical rectangle with two lines spiking up and down. The vertical rectangle is known as the *real body* and encompasses the trading activity between the opening and closing prices. For example, if the opening price is higher than the closing price, it will be recorded at the top of the real body and the closing price at the bottom. The vertical line above the body measures the distance between the high of the day and the higher of the opening or closing price. The lower line represents the distance between the low of the day and the lower of the opening or closing price. Days when

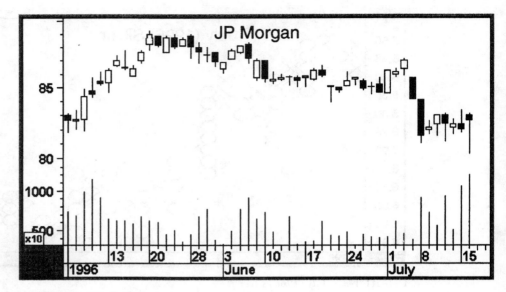

CHART 1-4. *J. P. Morgan.*

the close is higher than the opening are represented by transparent real bodies; days when the opening is higher than the close are displayed by a solid real body. Even though candles can be plotted for any period in which information is available, I use days in the example because daily candle charts are the most common.

Candle charts place greater emphasis on the opening and closing prices than do bar charts. One disadvantage of candles is that they take up a lot of horizontal space, so it's possible to plot only a small amount of data at a time. Fortunately, candle trend reversal signals are very short-term in nature. While candles are certainly no magic wand, they are a useful technical tool for short-term traders.

The candlestick charting method is detailed in Chapter Eleven. In this chapter we will focus our attention on bar and close-only charts.

Generally speaking, the term *charting* refers to charts that reflect price and/or volume, such as those just described. The term *technical analysis,* on the other hand, covers a much wider ground. It includes a host of indicators and techniques used in conjunction with the raw price and volume data. You may recall that our earlier definition of technical analysis included the expression "weight of the evidence" in describing trends. It is this arsenal of indicators that we use as evidence that a trend has or has not reversed. The analyses throughout this text will stress the weight of the evidence, because it's so very important to have as many indicators point in the same direction as possible. That way, we increase the probabilities of being correct. Unfortunately, we can never eliminate the probabilities of being wrong.

METHODS OF SCALING CHARTS

Prices in bar and line charts are displayed on the vertical, or Y, axis. There are two ways in which they are scaled: arithmetic or ratio (sometimes known as log or semilogarithmic). An arithmetic scale (Chart 1-5) plots each price differential with the same vertical distance. Thus, the distance between a price of $5 and $6 will be the same as that between $100 and $101.

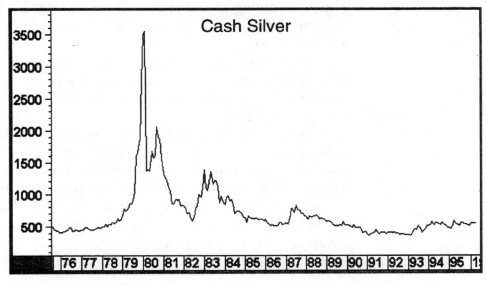

CHART 1-5. *Cash silver.*

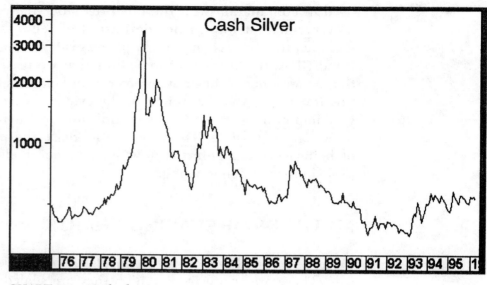

CHART 1-6.   *Cash silver.*

On the other hand, the ratio chart (Chart 1-6) allocates the same proportionate price swing the same vertical distance. Thus a doubling of the price will be represented by the same vertical distance (say, an inch), whether it's from $1 to $2 or $100 to $200.

On shorter-term charts, covering a time span of perhaps 2 to 3 months, it doesn't make much difference which scale is used, but for longer-term charts the difference can be, and often is, crucial.

Just consider a stock that sells at $4. A $1 fluctuation in either direction is a big move, yet the arithmetic method will give it the same importance even if the stock is trading at $50, where a $1 fluctuation is relatively minor. I will have more to say on the choice of scale in later chapters, but for now I would like to leave you with the idea that if you have a choice, always use the ratio or semilog scale.

SUMMARY

1. Prices in freely traded markets are determined by the attitudes toward the emerging fundamentals held by market participants and potential participants.
2. These attitudes evolve in trends.
3. The art of technical analysis is to identify trend changes at an early point and ride on the trend until the weight of the evidence points in the opposite direction.
4. There are four principal methods of charting: bar, close-only, point-and-figure, and candlestick.
5. There are two ways to scale a chart: arithmetic and ratio. Ratio is preferred, since changes in crowd psychology have a tendency to move in proportion and ratio charts reflect this phenomenon more accurately.

THE MARKET CYCLE MODEL AND BASIC TREND IDENTIFICATION

DIFFERENT TYPES OF TRENDS

In Chapter One we talked a lot about trends and the need to ride a trend until the weight of the evidence shows that it has reversed. In this chapter we will learn all about trends, which will put us in a better position to assess the significance of the various technical signals. However, before we can identify a trend reversal, we must know what a trend is.

Different types of trends are really different units of time span. Daily charts reflect very short-term trends lasting as little as a few days, whereas multidecade charts containing monthly data reflect trends of 5 to 10 years or more. This is an important distinction, for the longer a trend is in existence the greater the implications of its reversal once a signal has been given.

For practical purposes, there are four types of trends: short-term trends, of 3 to 6 weeks; intermediate-term trends, of 6 weeks to 9 months; primary trends, of 9 months to 2 years; and secular trends, comprised of several primaries, usually lasting 8 to 12 years. These are very rough guides, since time frames can and do differ from those I've given and should therefore be used as much for a relative as an absolute comparison.

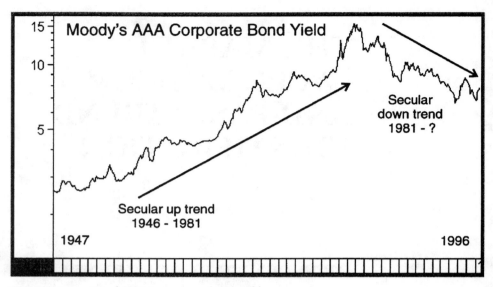

CHART 2-1.   *Moody's AAA corporate bond yield.*

The secular (very long-term) trend is not of much interest to short-term traders, but provides an important background for investors (Chart 2-1). Because secular trends last such a long time, they do not reverse direction very often. When they do, it is a very important event. I will explain why later.

The primary trend revolves around the so-called 4-year business cycle (Figure 2-1). It consists of a bull market, or primary uptrend, and a bear market, or primary downtrend. Primary trends can be as short as 6 months and as long as 3 years. Normally 12 to 18 months is a more accurate reflection of the time span. Also, bull trends have a tendency to be longer than bear trends (Chart 2-2) for any cycle. After all, it takes a longer time to build than to tear down.

Investors are principally concerned with the primary trend, because the secular trend is generally too long for the attention span of most people. Consequently, it is of the utmost importance to position assets in the direction of the main trend. It is also relevant for shorter-term traders to have some idea of the direction of the primary trend even though they may not "play" it as such. This is because a rising trend, like a rising tide, lifts all boats. Invariably, in mechanical trading sys-

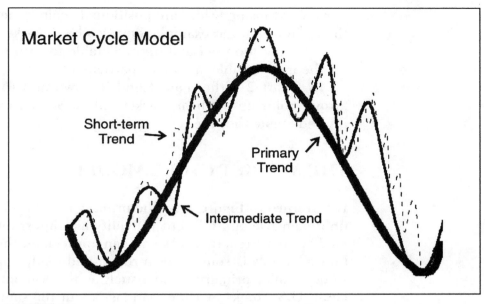

FIGURE 2-1.

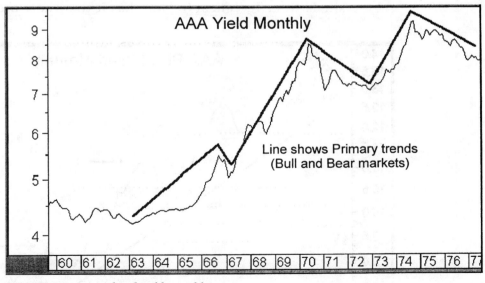

CHART 2-2. *AAA bond yield monthly.*

tems, most losing trades are positioned against the direction of the main trend. For example, during a bear market, the market rally is often too brief and unpredictable to earn profits except for the most nimble and lucky participants.

In Chart 2-3 the main trend is down and the horizontal arrows point up the bear market rallies. See how difficult and unpredictable they are.

THE MARKET CYCLE MODEL

Let's return to Figure 2-1. The primary trend is depicted as an unbroken rise and fall, but in reality it is interrupted by inter-mediate-term reactions. As you can appreciate, the categoriza-tion of trends is sometimes a rough-and-ready approximation, since smaller primary trends, such as the 8-month bear mar-ket in U.S. stocks in 1966, can last about the same time as an unusually long intermediate trend, though this is quite a rare occurrence.

In bull markets, intermediate rallies last longer and have greater magnitude than declines. In bear markets, the oppo-site is true. Technical folklore has it that there are three inter-

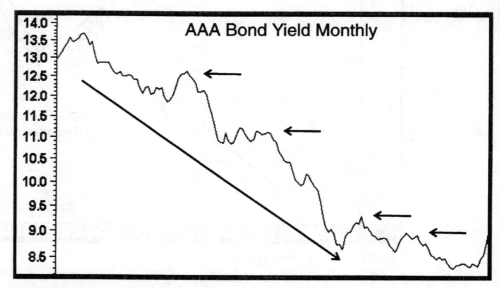

CHART 2-3. *AAA bond yield monthly.*

mediate cycles in a bull market. It is a generally accepted principle that a countercyclical move retraces between one-third and two-thirds of the previous move. In other words, the correction will normally retrace anywhere from one-third to two-thirds of the previous advance in a bull market, and vice versa in a bear market.

Finally, we bring in the short-term trends, as represented by the dashed lines. Short-term trends, which occasionally last as long as 6 weeks, tend to be much more influenced by random news events than the longer intermediate and primary trends and are therefore much more difficult to identify. Generally speaking, in a relative sense, the longer the trend, the easier it is to identify.

It should be apparent by now that prices at any one time are influenced by a confluence of trends. In this instance we are considering only three: short-term, intermediate-term, and primary. Clearly it is important for all market participants, with the possible exception of intraday traders, to at least attempt to determine the prevailing stage of the cycle. Investors, who typically have a long-term horizon of a year or more, need to know whether the primary trend has just begun, is at the middle, or has reached a very mature phase. It is obviously much better to be buying on the first or second short-term rally in the first intermediate upwave than on the top of the last intermediate and short-term rallies.

Short-term traders, on the other hand, need to make sure they are positioned in the direction of the primary trend. This is because surprises typically occur in the direction of the main or primary trend. Rallies go further in bull markets; declines can and will be precipitous in bear markets.

This *market cycle model* should form the heart of all your strategic analysis and thinking. It's far from perfect, but it will give you a framework on which to base your other analyses.

PEAK-AND-TROUGH ANALYSIS

One of the principal building blocks of technical analysis is the idea that prices do not move straight up or straight down, but experience zigzag movements, as shown in Figure 2-2. In an uptrend, a rally is interrupted by a correction, and is followed by another rally, then another correction retracing part of the upmove, and so on. These are the peaks and troughs, each peak being higher than its predecessor and each counter-cyclical decline ending at a progressively higher point. As long as this series of rising peaks and troughs is intact, the uptrend is assumed to be in force. However, when the price experiences a peak that is lower than the previous peak (point A), and the next reaction takes the price below the previous low (point B), this series of rising peaks and troughs is no longer in force—a signal that the trend has reversed. In Figure 2-2 the reversal is triggered at the arrow.

The transition from a bear or negative trend to a bull or positive one is illustrated in Figure 2-3. Again, we are looking to see when the series of declining peaks and troughs is reversed and a new trend of rising tops and bottoms begins. The actual low is at point A, which we can see quite clearly with the benefit of hindsight. The *confirmation* that this was indeed the low did not come until point D, as indicated by the arrow.

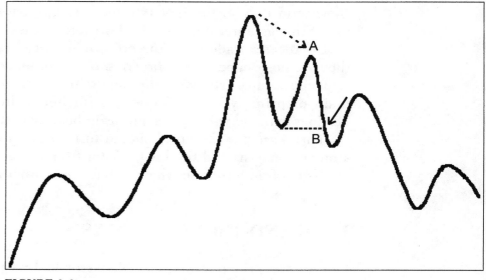

FIGURE 2-2.

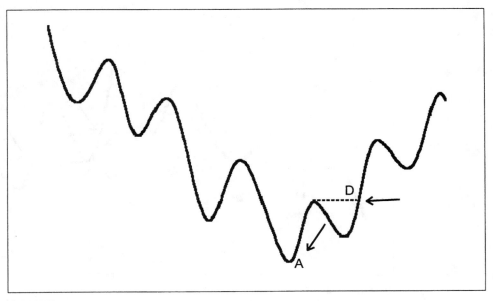

FIGURE 2-3.

A good analogy for the peak-and-trough concept is the change in the tide. If you go down to the beach and look at the water, initially you have no idea of the direction of the tide. It is only when you watch the wave action, noticing whether the waves are advancing or receding, that you can tell whether the tide is going out or coming in. As the tide stops going out, there is a period of indecision when it is not possible to discern a trend. But gradually one wave makes a 15-minute record high, and then another, until you can be sure that the tide has now turned and is at last coming in. Look for the same phenomenon in your charts and you'll be pleasantly surprised as to how useful this approach can be.

Few things in life are straightforward, and peak-and-trough analysis is no exception. Sometimes we are faced with a dilemma, as shown by the half-signal in Figure 2-4. Half-signals in a bull trend develop when the series of rising peaks remains intact, but the series of troughs does not. At point X, the low is lower than the previous low, but the previous peak, at point A, is still the highest in the trend.

Point X presents us with a dilemma, because the series of peaks is still intact but the market has already broken to a low.

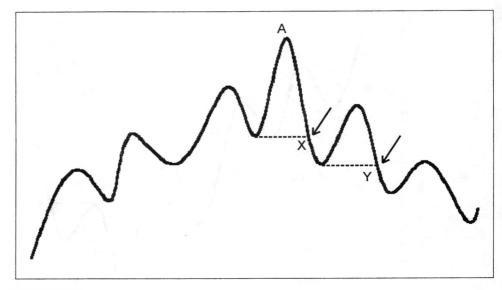

FIGURE 2-4.

Do we take the peaks as our reference and assume the uptrend is intact, or do we use the lower trough and call a turn in the tide? Strictly speaking, we should wait for a failed rally such as that shown in Figure 2-4 and then call a turn at point Y, when it is clear that the series of rising peaks *and* troughs have *both* been reversed.

Having said that, I prefer to look at point X as a half-signal in our weight-of-the-evidence trend reversal interpretation. This means that if other technical evidence is overwhelmingly bearish, we should go bearish at point X. Remember, we are dealing in probabilities, so the greater the evidence, the stronger the possibility that the trend is reversing.

The exact opposite situation for the peak-and-trough dilemma is shown in Figure 2-5, as the price reverses from a bear to a bull trend. This time, point X occurs when the series of declining peaks has been reversed, but not the declining troughs, and point Y occurs when they have both been reversed.

HOW SIGNIFICANT IS THE REVERSAL?

The importance of these peak-and-trough signals will depend on the trends they are reflecting. A primary-trend peak will be

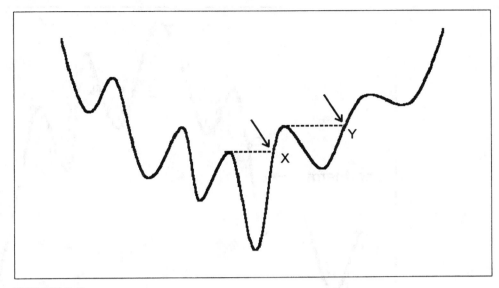

FIGURE 2-5.

signaled by a reversal in the trend of intermediate peaks and troughs, as we saw in Figure 2-1. Intermediate bottoms will be signaled by a reversal in the declining trend of short-term peaks and troughs, as shown in Figure 2-6.

Now we get to look at a couple of examples in the marketplace. Chart 2-4 features the cash Swiss franc as traded on the international money market (IMM). This is a close-only or line chart using weekly data. The A lines represent primary bull markets; line B indicates a bear trend. Immediately you can see that the 3-year bull trend between 1985 and late 1987 falls well out of the normal bull market time span of 1 to 2 years. I have purposely pointed this out to demonstrate that the guidelines we looked at earlier are just that: *guidelines*. Many trends can and do fall out of that range.

The bull market does exhibit one important principle, that of rising peaks and troughs. If you look at the A lines carefully, you will see that each of the rallies and reactions is above its predecessor, until early 1988, when the signals appear for the new bear market as far as this particular indicator is concerned. Since this is a weekly chart, it is not easy to discern the difference between a short and intermediate rally or reac-

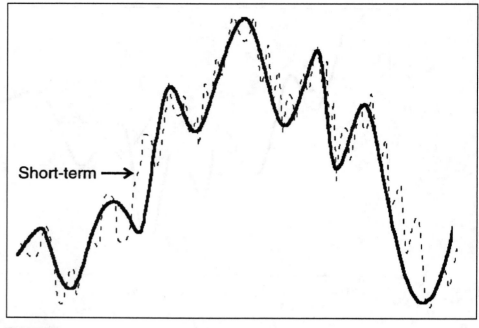

FIGURE 2-6.

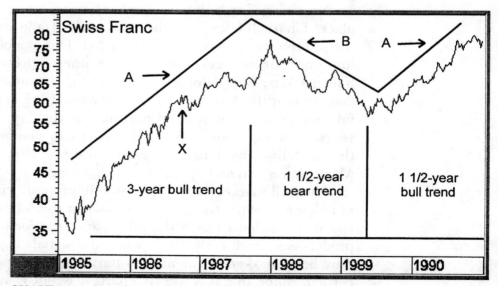

CHART 2-4.   *Swiss franc and 3-year bull trend.*

tion. Is the sharp decline in mid-1985 a short-or intermediate-term reaction? It looks more like a short-term one to me, since it only took about 2 weeks to complete. The reaction in late 1986 has more of the feeling of a small intermediate trend, since it lasted about 6 weeks. Also, it was interrupted by a short-term rally at point X.

One thing is clear, and that is the principle of positioning yourself against the main trend. If you had put on short positions in anticipation of any of the corrections, you would have had your head handed to you on a platter—unless you were unusually nimble. On the other hand, it would have been difficult for you to lose money from the long side, because the rallies that went in the direction of the main trend were strong and the reactions weak. Again, a rising tide lifts all boats. The rising primary bull market certainly did in this instance.

As you can see, the bear market in 1988 was more typical. The time span of 18 months fit the average. Also, it experienced five waves down: an initial intermediate decline; a short-term rally, which really took the form of a sideways congestion movement; another intermediate decline; a sharp bear market rally; and a final intermediate decline to the bear market low.

The next bull market in 1989 and 1990 also fell within the normal time span, but was closer to the previous bull market in terms of form—that is, very mild bull market corrections.

Chart 2-5 shows GATX Corporation. The first bull market experienced the normal five-wave up affair: intermediate rally, short-term reaction, another rally, a small reaction, and a final intermediate rally to the bull market peak.

The subsequent bear market also unfolded in a fairly normal way: intermediate decline, bear market rally, large intermediate decline, short-term rally, and final intermediate plunge. See how it was signaled by a failure of the price to make a new high in early 1990, then a break below the late-1989 low. Up to that point the series of rising bottoms and tops was still in force.

The 1990–91 bull market lasted for only 10 months, but still exhibited a condensed five-wave format. Up to that point things had unfolded in as classic a textbook format as we

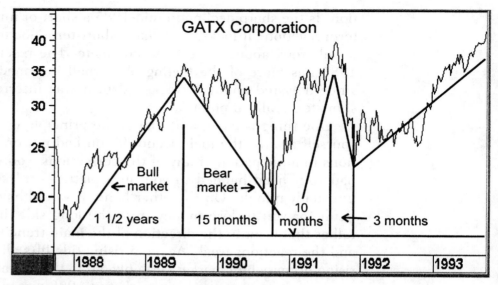

CHART 2-5. *GATX Corporation and bull/bear trend.*

could hope to get. Then a new decline set in. There was really no signaling point so far as peak-and-trough analysis is concerned, since no intermediate peak occurred. Also, the 3-month decline fell well short of the normal bear market benchmarks. I originally labeled this as a bear market, but after studying it a bit more since, I came to the conclusion that the decline fit better under the intermediate banner. The 40 percent price drop is certainly characteristic of a bear market. However, the 3-month duration falls well within the normal range of intermediate time spans, and well out of the primary-trend range. Second, the price retraced less than two-thirds of its previous advance, again within typical intermediate-trend parameters.

SUMMARY

1. Three principal types of trends are followed by investors and traders: short-term, intermediate-term, and long-term (primary) trends.

2. The secular, or very long-term, trend is also useful for longer-term investors.

3. Both investors and short-term traders should try to determine the direction and maturity of the primary trend.

4. Peak-and-trough analysis is a major building block of technical analysis and a basic trend identification technique.

SUPPORT AND RESISTANCE

DEFINITION

Two terms you hear a lot about are *support* and *resistance*. Basically, they are points on a chart where the probabilities favor at least a temporary halt in the prevailing trend. For example, if prices are declining and reach support, as in Figure 3-1, they can normally be expected to bounce. The rally may be temporary, as at point A, or may even mark the low point for the whole move, as at point B. The objective of this chapter is to cover the characteristics of these support and resistance areas and to learn their significance.

In their classic book *Technical Analysis of Stock Trends*, Edwards and Magee define support as *buying, actual or potential, sufficient in volume to halt a downtrend in prices for an appreciable period.* While we're on the subject of definitions, resistance is *selling, actual or potential, sufficient in volume to satisfy all bids and hence stop prices going higher for a time.*

Think of resistance as a temporary ceiling and support as a temporary floor, as illustrated in Figure 3-2. In order to become a floor, a support area must represent a concentration of demand. I emphasize the word *concentration*, because supply and demand, by definition, are always in balance. At whatever price a stock trades, there will always be the same amount bought as is sold. It is the relative concentration or enthusiasm of either buyers or sellers that determines the price level. A support area, then, is one in which sellers become less enthusiastic or less willing to part with their

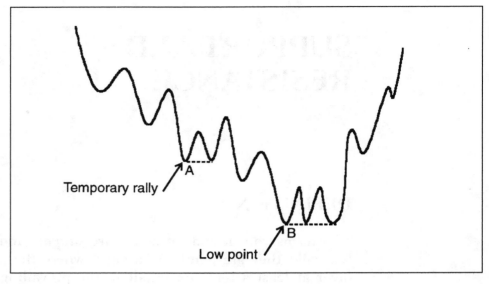

Temporary rally

A

Low point

B

FIGURE 3-1.

assets and buyers, at least temporarily, are more strongly motivated.

Often support and resistance areas occur at round numbers. For the Dow in the 1970s, it was 1000. Every time the Dow came up against that psychologically important number, sellers became more enthusiastic and prices declined. For gold in the mid-1980s and 1990s, the magic number has been $400.

Perhaps the best way to explain how support and resistance work is to look at the theoretical example in Figure 3-3. Let's say a stock price is initially in a downtrend and finds support at Point A1, which happens to be $25—a nice round number. You can also see there is a great amount of stock changing hands there. Even so, the decline is only temporarily halted, and prices begin to slip once again, until they reach point B1. Support at B1 is a little more formidable, since it forms the lower end of a temporary trading range. It's actually a rectangle. Once again, though, the price eventually slips to a new low as the enthusiasm of buyers is overwhelmed by the sellers.

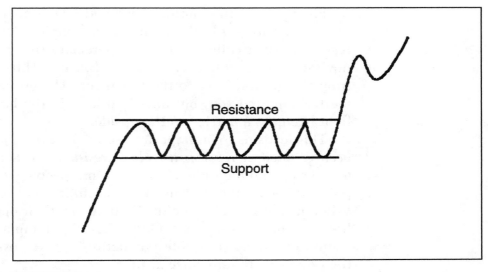

FIGURE 3-2.

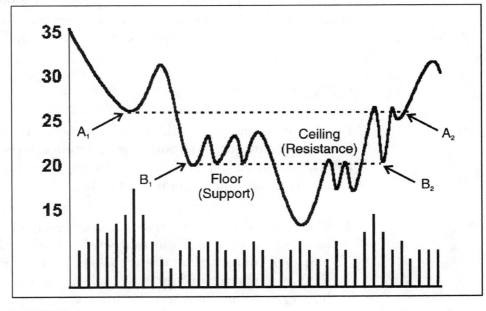

FIGURE 3-3.

Finally, the price bottoms out and begins to work its way higher. If you think of support as a floor in a building and resistance as a ceiling, you can appreciate that a floor at B1 now reverses its role to a ceiling at B2. It's a little like falling from the ground floor to the basement. The ground floor formerly supported you, but once you land in the basement, the floor becomes a barrier on the upside.

This leads us to an important rule: *Once a support zone has been violated, it reverses its role to resistance when prices start to rally again.* One rationale here is that people who bought at point B1 watched as the price of their stock plummeted. When it rallied back to point B2, they saw their opportunity to break even, and they sold. Only when this temporary concentration of supply (to quote our definition) was overcome was the price able to rally once again.

In addition, price finds resistance at point A2. Remember, this is where a lot of stock changed hands, so again a lot of people wanted to break even. Not surprisingly, when the price starts to retreat once more, it finds support at point B2. Once again, we find that the price level reverses its role from *resistance* on the way up to *support* on the way down.

GENERAL RULES

I am sure you are now asking the question, "How do I know how important each support and resistance level is likely to be?" Unfortunately, I can't answer that question precisely, but I can offer you some general rules to help.

1. *The more of a security that changes hands at a particular level, the more significant that level is likely to be as a support or resistance zone* (Figure 3-4). That is fairly self-evident, for whenever you have a large number of people buying or selling at a specific price they tend to remember their own experiences. Buyers, as we discovered, like to break even after suffering a loss. Sellers, on the other

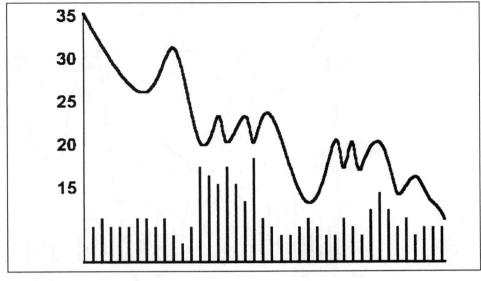

FIGURE 3-4.

hand, may have bought lower down and now recall that prices previously stalled at the resistance area. Therefore, their motivation for taking profits is that much greater.

2. *The greater the speed of the preceding price movement, the more significant a support or resistance zone is likely to be* (Figure 3-5).   Just think of trying to lift a heavy weight. If you make the attempt after running a fast race, you are less likely to succeed than someone who has not made such a dash. Markets are the same way. A modest support or resistance barrier is likely to be much more significant if prices have been racing ahead or declining sharply than if prices are reached after a slow steady advance or decline.

3. *The more powerful the move preceding the support or resistance zone, the greater its potential as a barrier* (Figure 3-6). This may seem to contradict the previous rule but it does not. It is important to make a distinction between a speedy and lengthy move and a powerful one. Remember our analogy to lifting a weight after running a fast race. Well, if the

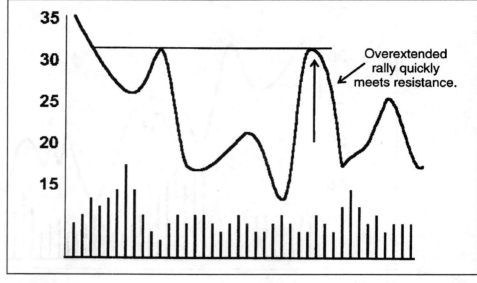

FIGURE 3-5.

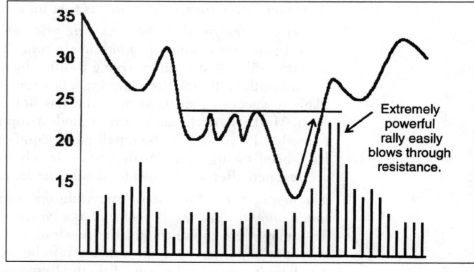

FIGURE 3-6.

lifter is normal, the rule still stands. However, if an Olympic athlete has just run the race, lifting the weight will be a piece of cake. It works the same way in the marketplace. An area of resistance, for example, will quickly fall if the previous move is associated with a huge expansion of volume and momentum. If there is a lot of power behind a move, the support or resistance zone is much more likely to fall on the first attempt.

4. *The more times a support or resistance zone has been able to halt or reverse a price trend in the past, the greater its significance is likely to be* (Figure 3-7).   Recall our example of a building. The more times a floor is pounced on but does not give way, the greater the implication when the floor finally does give way. This is probably the single most important rule we have for estimating the potential importance of a support or resistance area. Just think again of the Dow Jones Industrial Average: From 1966 to 1982, 1000 was the barrier to beat. It had been touched on several occasions but never decisively breached. Once 1000 was bettered, the move to 2, 3, 4, and 5000 came relatively easily.

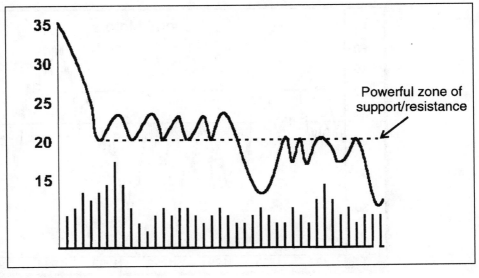

FIGURE 3-7.

5. *The longer the period that has elapsed between the time a support or resistance zone was last challenged, the less significance it is likely to have.* This means that a supply which is 6 months old is likely to have greater potency than one established 10 or 20 years ago. Even so, it is almost uncanny how support and resistance levels can repeat their effectiveness time and time again, even when separated by many years.

EXAMPLES

Chart 3-1 shows some support and resistance lines for General Motors Corporation. The lower line, at about $44, indicates that this form of analysis is by no means an exact science. The $44 level certainly acted as excellent resistance in 1991 and 1992, and again in January 1995. It also acted as support in late 1995. However, it definitely failed the principle that a resistance area reverses its role to one of support when it was temporarily penetrated in 1993.

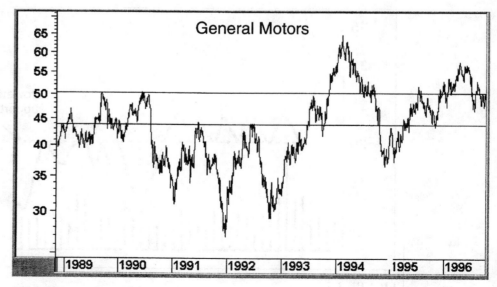

CHART 3-1. *General Motors.*

The upper line occurred at a round number of $50. See how it acted as resistance in late 1989, early 1990, and again in mid-1993. This level even acted as temporary support in the 1994 decline, since prices hung around $50 for about 2 months. Finally, the mid-1995 rally was temporarily halted at $50. All lines were useful, up to a point. However, they all demonstrate that just because a level was formerly a support or resistance area does not mean that prices can always be expected to reverse their trend. The level is merely an intelligent place to expect a reversal.

Chart 3-2 shows the Dow Jones World Stock Index, excluding the U.S. market. The lower line, at 117, is a good support and resistance example, since the late-1994 rally was reversed at the line and the two reactions in late June and October 1995 both found support there. Even the two reactions in May and early June 1995 were turned back just as they approached the line.

The next line, at 124, represented huge resistance on the way up in mid-1995. Then the line reversed its role of resistance to one of support twice in early 1996. Finally, the 128

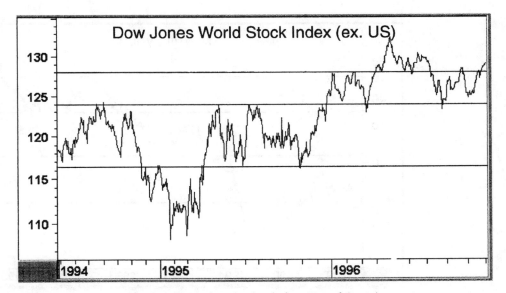

CHART 3-2. *Dow Jones World Stock Index (excluding United States).*

level acted as both resistance and support in late 1995 and early 1996. You can also appreciate from this chart that while a support or resistance zone can act as a temporary turning point for prices, it does not give any indication of how long or how large the new trend will be. For example, the 124 level served as resistance in August 1994, but only a small decline of about 2 points followed. Then a large decline developed in October, taking the index to 117. Finally, the market made two attempts to touch the line in late October, and these were followed by a huge decline to 113.

Chart 3-3, of Merrill Lynch, shows some interesting phenomena. First, the lower line acted as support in 1989, and then twice acted as resistance in 1990. The rally off the lows was quite a large one, and it would normally be reasonable to expect that the resistance line at $13 would act as a temporary barrier. The price must have been pretty exhausted after this sharp rally. However, volume (which is not shown) expanded considerably on the rally.

Later on we see some good examples of lines that kept changing their roles. The next one up, at $22, acted as resis-

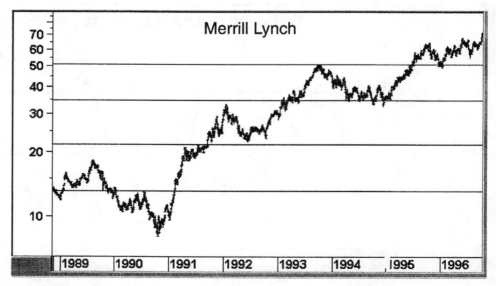

CHART 3-3. *Merrill Lynch.*

tance in 1991, then as support in 1992. The $35 barrier was even more impressive. It halted the 1992 rally and all the 1994–1995 declines. Finally, the round number of $50 again proved to be a useful support and resistance area, since it first turned back a rally in 1993 and then acted as support in 1996.

SUMMARY

1. Support and resistance zones are places on the chart where price trends are temporarily or permanently reversed.

2. Support and resistance zones often occur at round numbers.

3. There are five basic rules for assessing the probable importance of support and resistance areas: the amount of an asset that changes hands; the speed of the preceding price trend; the power of a preceding trend; the number of times a zone has been able to halt rallies and reactions; and the length of time that has elapsed since the zone was previously attacked.

TREND INDICATORS

In Part One we learned that prices move in trends, and that the objective of technical analysis is to identify those trend changes at a relatively early stage and ride on the trend until the weight of the evidence proves beyond a reasonable doubt that it has reversed again. Part Two looks in greater detail at the pieces of evidence and the various techniques that help identify changes in trend. This is really the heart and soul of the technical approach, and you will find yourself using these tools over and over again.

PRICE PATTERNS

When you look at price charts, you rarely find that prices reverse on a dime (Figure 4-1). A reversal from an uptrend to a downtrend is usually separated by some volatile trading-range activity in which buyers and sellers experience a closely fought battle. During the rally phase, buyers have the upper hand over sellers, since it is their enthusiasm that pushes up prices. During the transitional phase, the enthusiasm of buyers and sellers becomes more balanced as neither is able to win out over the other. Finally, sellers predominate and prices begin a new downtrend. It's important to note that it is not the number of buyers or sellers that changes, but the relative balance in their enthusiasm. After all, every purchase must, by definition, be offset by a sale. However, if sellers are fearful, they are more anxious to sell and are more willing to accept a

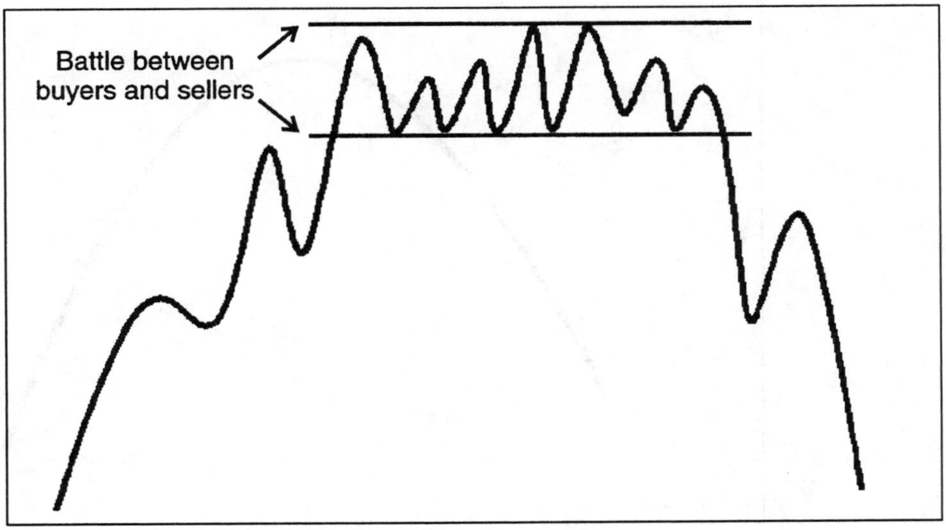

Battle between
buyers and sellers

FIGURE 4-1.

lower price, and vice versa. Over the years, technicians have noticed that these battles are reflected in the charts by clearly identifiable patterns or formations. Understanding what the patterns are and their characteristics is what this chapter is all about.

Figure 4-2 shows prices moving straight up and then straight down, but this is rarely the case in the actual marketplace. Straight movement is possible, when markets become highly emotional, as in the 1929 top in the stock market, but it is the exception, not the rule. A more likely scenario is that shown in Figure 4-1, in which the uptrend is separated from the downtrend by some ranging action.

RECTANGLES

The pattern that most clearly demonstrates this temporary balance between buyers and sellers in the transition period is the rectangle. Figure 4-3 shows the tail end of a long rally, following which prices move back and forth in a trading range. The

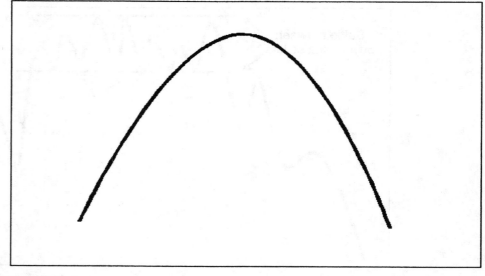

FIGURE 4-2.

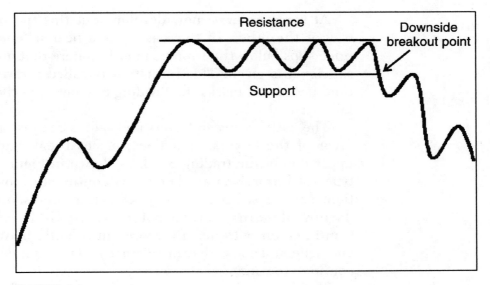

FIGURE 4-3.

rectangle is constructed by drawing two horizontal lines marking the top and bottom boundaries of the trading range. The lines join the rally peaks and reaction lows. These are known as support and resistance areas, or support and resistance zones. The upper line represents resistance, because prices experience a barrier to any further upside movement. It is a place where sellers are anxious to sell because they are obtaining good price, and where buyers are less willing to bid up prices because they feel things have gotten too expensive. When the resistance line is touched the first time, the relative balance between buyers and sellers tips to the sellers. After a while, the buyers are more enthusiastic about making purchases (the first time the lower line is touched). Sellers, remembering the higher prices they could have received at the upper line, are, at the margin, prepared to hold off for a while in the hope that prices will rise. The price at the lower line is therefore said to be at support. Because of this change in sentiment, prices again rise until they reach the vicinity of the upper line, and the whole process begins again.

At some point, a new development tips the balance one way or the other. In this case it is a bearish one, since the price slips below the support line. It is here that a trend reversal signal is given. This formation is called a reversal formation, because it marks the dividing line between the rising and falling trend.

The battle between buyers and sellers can just as well go in favor of the buyers. If it does, prices break out above the upper end of the trading band, as shown in Figure 4-4. These types of formations are known as continuation or consolidation rectangles, because the price action represents a consolidation of gains before prices work their way higher. Continuation patterns still represent a battle between buyers and sellers, it's just that in this particular instance the buyers continue to win.

The same principles apply in the transition from a downtrend to an uptrend. Figure 4-5 shows a reversal rectangle as the bearish trend is reversed in favor of a bullish one. Figure 4-6 shows a consolidation rectangle during a downward trend. Generally speaking, it is a technical principle that a trend is

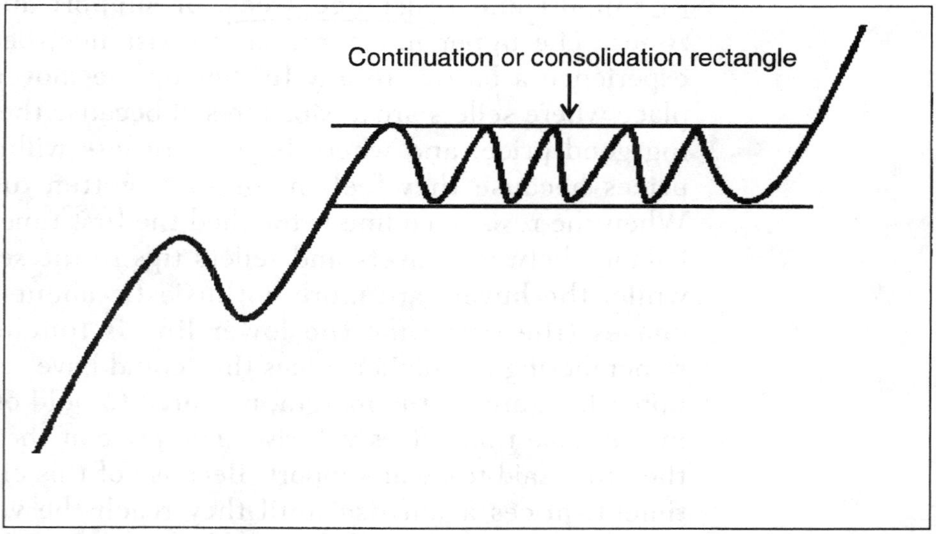

Continuation or consolidation rectangle

FIGURE 4-4.

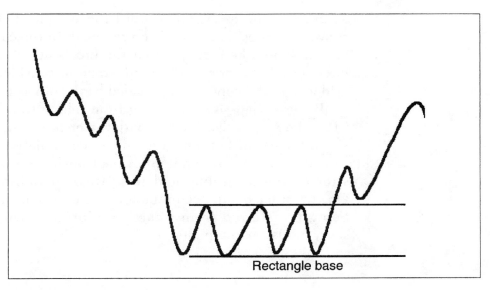

Rectangle base

FIGURE 4-5.

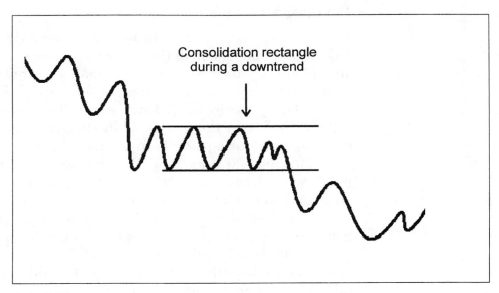

Consolidation rectangle
during a downtrend

FIGURE 4-6.

assumed to be in existence until the weight of the evidence shows or proves that it has been reversed. In the case of rectangles, it should be assumed that the breakout will occur in the direction of the prevailing trend—that is, providing no strong evidence to the contrary is provided by the other indicators.

Patterns that separate rising from falling trends (Figure 4-7) are known as distribution patterns or tops, and their opposite numbers at bottoms are called accumulation patterns or formations. Distribution implies the transfer of a security from strong, knowledgeable holders to weak or uninformed ones. On the other hand, accumulation occurs when the security is being transferred from weak, uninformed owners to more savvy market participants.

FOUR BASIC PRINCIPLES OF PATTERN INTERPRETATION

PATTERN SIGNIFICANCE

Price patterns take on significance from their size and depth. Other things being equal, the larger the pattern, the greater its significance. Chart 4-1 shows a small rectangle in a daily chart; note how the reversal lasts for only a short period. Remember, patterns are a battleground between buyers and sellers. The bigger the battle and the longer it takes, the more exhausted the losing side becomes and the greater the implication for the new price move. You can see that Chart 4-1 is a much larger formation, lasting many months, and the ensuing trend is therefore more significant.

If a bull trend has been in force for a couple of years, it is going to take a much greater change in psychology to reverse it; consequently, it will require a much longer battle between buyers and sellers than a transition period following a 3-week rally. Think of the amount of energy needed to reverse a fully loaded freight train compared with just reversing the engine itself.

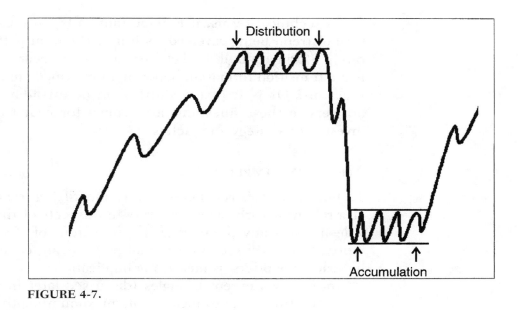

FIGURE 4-7.

CHART 4-1. *India growth.*

In technical terms, it is important to try to recognize the type of trend being reversed. Is it a distribution pattern separating a primary bull market from a primary bear market? Or is it a transition formation between an intermediate rally and a reaction? Or is it just a short-term or intraday top? The answers to these questions are crucial for your trading and investment strategy and tactics.

MEASURING IMPLICATIONS

Technical analysis is concerned with identifying trend changes at a relatively early stage, but very few aspects of this art provide us with any pointers as to the extent of the expected move. As we will see later, not all patterns are created equal, but each one offers us measuring implications.

In all cases except triangles (discussed later in the chapter), the principle is to measure its maximum depth and project this distance from the breakout point. For a rectangle, the maximum distance is the space that separates the two parallel lines (lines A and B in Figure 4-8). Then project that distance

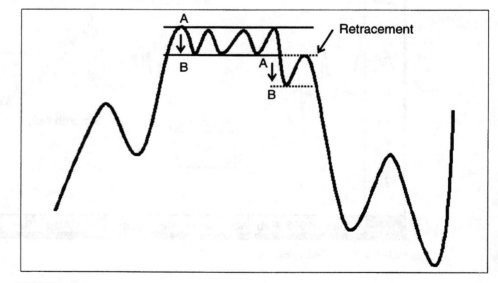

FIGURE 4-8.

on the downside, because this is a top formation. One important thing to remember about breakouts is that they are, in many cases, followed by retracement moves, which take the price either toward the pattern or to its outer extremity. Figure 4-8 shows a full retracement to the pattern and extended lower horizontal line.

The same measuring technique is used at market bottoms, as in the case of the accumulation pattern shown in Figure 4-9. Now you can see that the depth of the pattern is important, because the larger the depth the greater the size of the indicated new trend. This leads us to another important question, the choice of arithmetic or ratio scale (see Chapter One) for the Y, or price, axis of the chart. To recap, in an arithmetic or linear scaling, each vertical distance represents the same amount of price change. In Figure 4-10, each arrow represents a vertical move of one point.

Figure 4-11, on the other hand, reflects a ratio or semilog scaling in which each arrow represents the same proportionate move—namely, a doubling in price. In very short-term

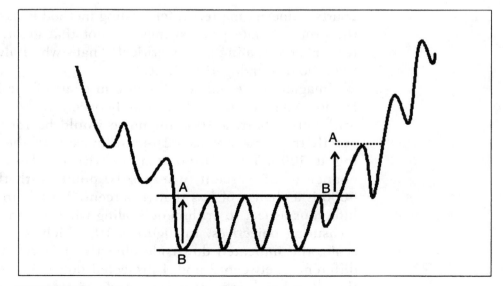

FIGURE 4-9.

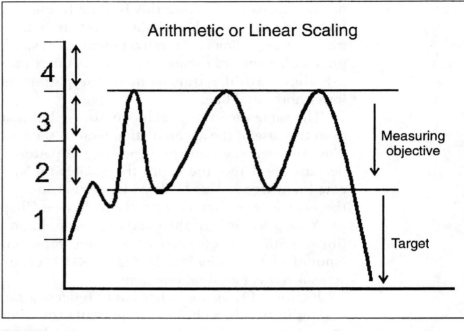

FIGURE 4-10.

charts it doesn't matter which scaling method is used, because the proportionate price swings are not that great. In longer-term charts, scaling is very critical. That's why I always prefer the ratio or semilogarithmic scale.

Imagine, for example, a long-term chart of the DJIA starting in 1932, when the level was between 40 and 50. On an arithmetic chart, a 10-point move would be represented in exactly the same way as a 10-point move with the DJIA trading at 5000. Yet a 10-point move with the Dow at 40 is a change of 25 percent, whereas 10 points with the Dow at 5000 is a change of less than 1 percent. There's an even more ludicrous aspect to arithmetic scaling when it comes to price-measuring objectives. In Figure 4-10, which is in arithmetic scale, the indicated downside objective is zero—that is, the difference between 2 and 4 projected down. Figure 4-11, on the other hand, is in ratio scale and indicates a more realistic

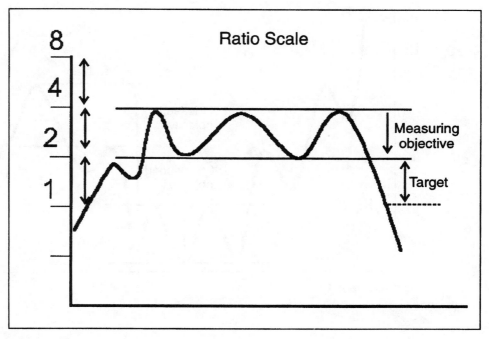

FIGURE 4-11.

downside of the *proportionate* distance between 2 and 4—
namely, a 50 percent decline to 1.

It has always been my assumption that market prices are a
function of psychological attitudes toward the emerging fundamentals. Since these moods have a tendency to move proportionately, it makes sense to plot them proportionately.

As noted earlier, price objectives drawn from patterns are
ultimate minimum objectives. The minimum is important,
because prices can, and often do, move in excess of the objective. Indeed, bearing in mind the idea that prices move in proportion, look at Figure 4-12, which shows that the price move
following the breakout was actually twice the indicated minimum. Multiples of the objective are obviously very important—not only as straight price objectives but because they
often serve as key pivotal points. In this respect, you can see
that the retracement found support at the approximate dis-

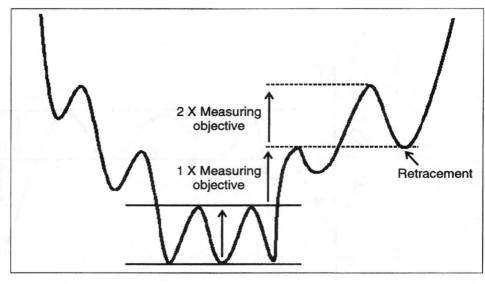

FIGURE 4-12.

tance of the minimum objective. Remember, the objectives are just as valid for continuation as for reversal patterns. It's also important to bear in mind that the price objective is not necessarily achieved in one move (Figure 4-13). It is an ultimate objective. Far too often investors enter a position expecting the price to rally straight to the measuring objective, only to find that the initial breakout is followed by a retracement move (Figure 4-13, point X to point Y) and that only during the subsequent rally is the objective achieved. Measuring objectives are concerned not only with magnitude, but with how long investors should expect to see a move perpetuate once a trend has reversed. Unfortunately, there are no hard-and-fast rules. Indeed, in many instances the indicated measuring objective of a move is not achieved. What we can say, though, is that the trend reversal should be assumed to be in force until the price and volume action provides sufficient evidence to the contrary. Figure 4-14 shows a rectangle top, a quick achievement of a downside objective, and then the formation of another rectangle—but this time a bullish rever-

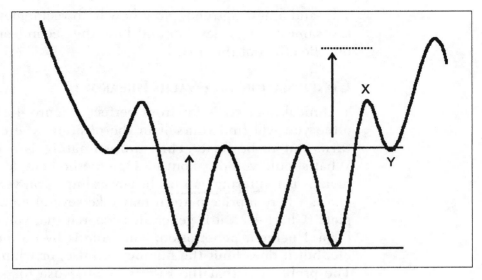

FIGURE 4-13.

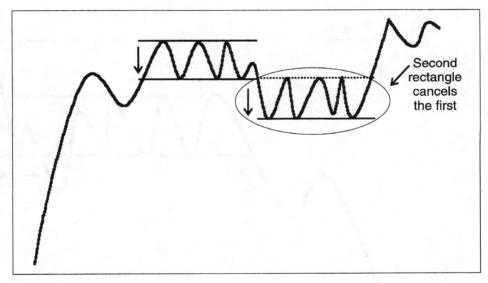

FIGURE 4-14.

sal—and a new uptrend. Note how both rectangles took about the same time to develop and how the second one canceled out the effect of the first.

CONFIRMATION OF A VALID BREAKOUT

Technical analysis is far from perfect (Figure 4-15), so quite often you will find yourself in the position where a breakout turns out to be false. This, unfortunately, is a fact of life. What should you do about it? One method employed by technicians is a filtering approach. For example, on very long-term charts where a price pattern may take several months to complete (Chart 4-2), it is generally accepted that you should wait for a 3 percent penetration. This rule is by no means infallible, but it does limit the number of false, or whipsaw signals. The problem is that the rule is of little use for shorter-term trends, in which 3 percent can often encompass the entire move. We will pick up some more hints for spotting valid breakouts in the next section, which is concerned with the significance of price patterns as affected by volume. For the time

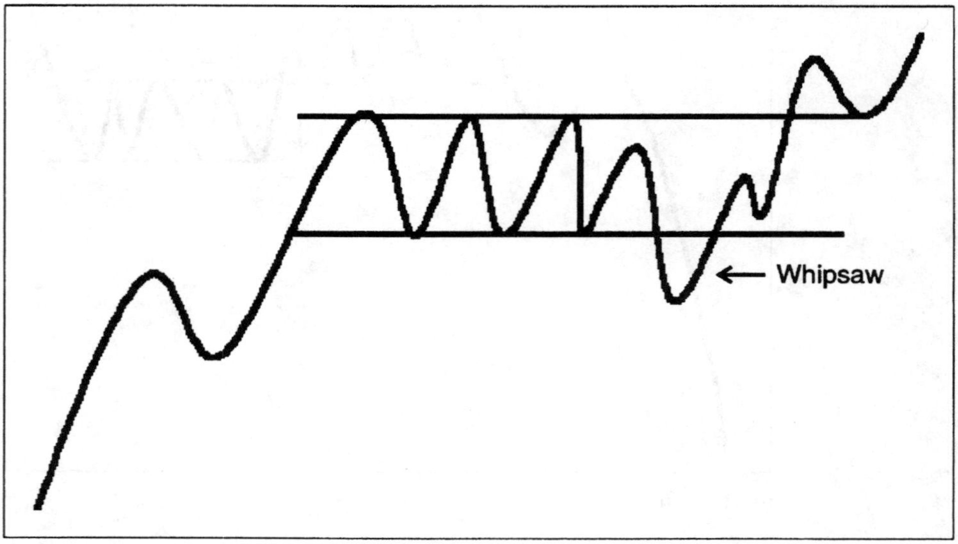

FIGURE 4-15.

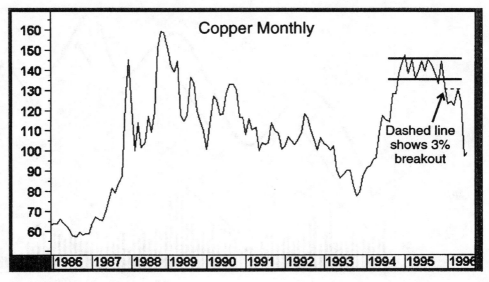

CHART 4-2. *Copper monthly.*

being, the answer lies in a case-by-case, commonsense approach.

VOLUME

It is very important to remember that *volume goes with the trend*. This means it is normal for volume to increase along with prices and to decrease as prices decline (Figure 4-16). Volume in technical analysis is always relative to the recent past.

When volume is going with the trend (i.e., moving in the direction of prices), it is telling us one thing and one thing only: The prevailing trend is healthy so far as this relationship is concerned. In Figure 4-16, the arrows during the zigzag up indicate this "in gear" relationship between volume and price. On the other hand, arrows A and B, during the bear market, show volume going against the trend, which is bearish. It is when volume moves against the trend that a warning is given.

In rising markets it is normal for volume to peak in the early

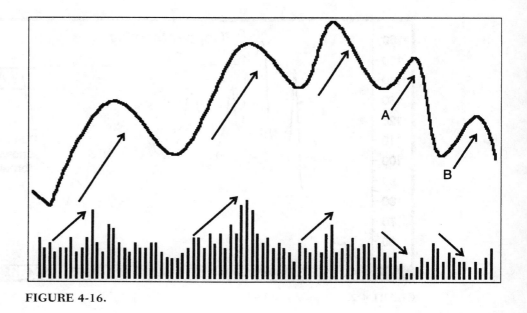

FIGURE 4-16.

to middle stages of a price pattern development. For example, in the case of a rectangle, it is often possible to draw a declining line above the volume bars, as in Figure 4-17, until activity almost shrinks to nothing. Then, as the price breaks on the upside, so should volume. This trend of declining volume is reflective of the fine balance between the enthusiasm of buyers and sellers that occurs at the end of the pattern. As prices get ready to advance, the expansion of volume tells us two things. First, the buyers have won. Second, there is a change in the psychology toward great enthusiasm—and you need enthusiasm to get a meaningful rally. A breakout that occurs with small volume is suspect, since it does not indicate this change in psychology. In Figure 4-18, the price is ready to break out on the upside—but as it does, look at the volume. There is clearly no sign of any enthusiasm. It is not surprising, therefore, that prices then move to the downside with a vengeance.

When prices are declining, it is normal for volume to decline as well. This means that downside breakouts from

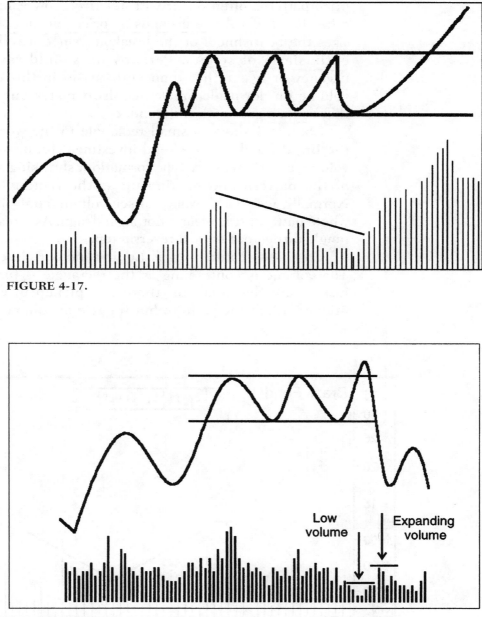

FIGURE 4-17.

FIGURE 4-18.

price patterns often occur with relatively low volume. On the other hand, if volume expands as prices decline, this emphasizes the bearishness of the breakout, since it reflects greater enthusiasm of sellers. Perhaps we should say it reflects urgency or fear rather than enthusiasm in this case. Rising volume on downside breakouts also violates our golden rule that volume goes with the trend.

Chart 4-3 shows a small rectangle in the weekly chart of the Brazil Fund, a closed-end investment fund. Note how the volume experiences a V-type formation, shrinking at the center of the pattern and picking up as the rectangle develops. Normally, we would expect to see volume controlled over the whole pattern. It is clearly not a good sign. As a result, the rectangle turned out to be a reversal top.

Chart 4-4 features Brazil Equity, another closed-end fund. The volume is contracting as the rectangle is formed. Then, just before the breakout, there is a pickup in volume. The price is still in the pattern, but the rise in volume as the price

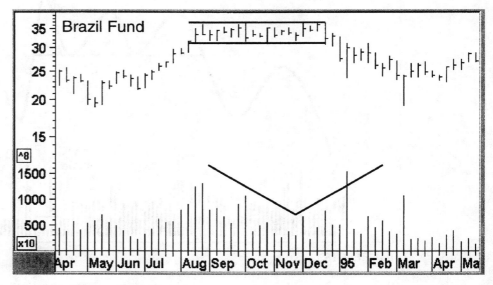

CHART 4-3. *Brazil Fund.*

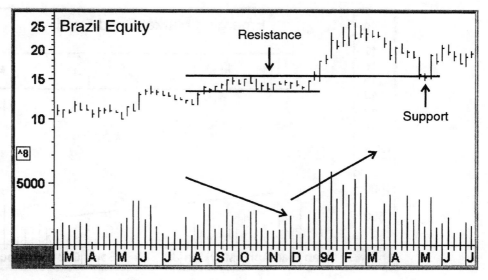

CHART 4-4. *Brazil Equity.*

advances is a good sign. The next week is a giveaway, as the price rallies above the resistance line on a very strong volume increase. The next couple of weeks also show heavy volume. It is worth noting that when the upper line is extended, the price falls back to the top of the pattern.

In Chart 4-5, the volume decreases as the rectangle is formed. The price slips below the lower boundary, but the break is never decisive, then. As the price rallies back above the lower parallel line, volume decreases—which is not a good sign. Finally, the rally gives way to a reaction, and prices slip once again. But this time volume expands—again a bearish sign, which is confirmed by a nasty downside move.

Chart 4-6 is another consolidation rectangle, this time in an uptrend. See how the volume tips us off as to which way the price is going to break. In the next period, all hell breaks loose on the upside as price and volume both explode.

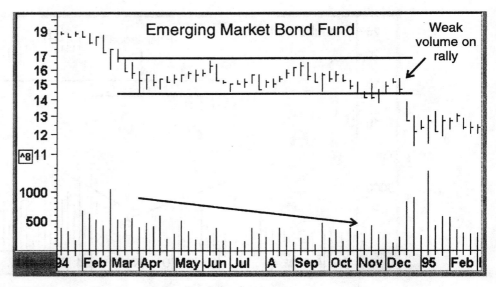

CHART 4-5.   *Emerging Market Bond Fund.*

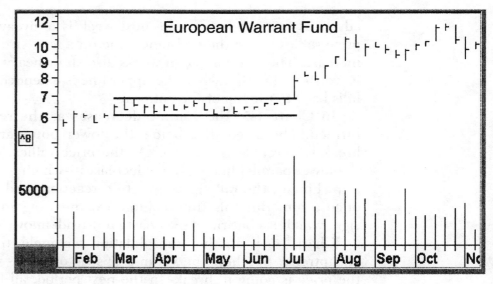

CHART 4-6.   *European Warrant Fund.*

HEAD-AND-SHOULDERS FORMATIONS

TOPS

Head and shoulders are one of the most common and certainly the most notorious of the various price patterns. These patterns occur as reversals, both up and down, and as continuation or consolidation formations.

The classic head and shoulders is shown in Figure 4-19. It consists of the final rally, the head, separated by two smaller (though not necessarily identical) rallies, known as the left and right shoulders. It is possible to construct a trendline joining the low of the left shoulder and the head. This is known as the neckline. The pattern is completed when the price breaks decisively below the neckline.

If you recall our discussion in the section on peak-and-trough analysis, you can now appreciate that the violation of the neckline is also a signal that the rising series of peaks and

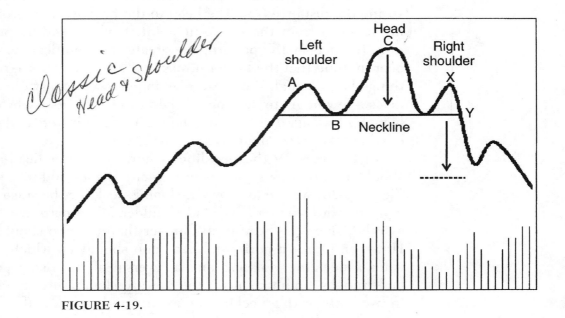

Classic Head & Shoulder

FIGURE 4-19.

troughs which preceded the formation of the head and shoulders has been reversed. The failed or lower peak is at X, and Y marks the breaking of the preceding low. The violation at point Y confirms that a series of declining peaks and troughs is now in force. As we will see later, this peak-and-trough technical building block forms the basis of several price patterns.

The all-important thing to watch for is that volume on the left shoulder, and sometimes the head, should be noticeably heavier than that associated with the right shoulder. In fact, the right shoulder is the first rally in the new bear trend, so you should expect the right-shoulder rally to be somewhat anemic, and for volume to contract as the price works its way higher. The other point to observe is that the retracement rally, if there is one, should be associated with low and declining volume. The initial breakdown from the pattern in Figure 4-19 is associated with a selling climax, as volume reaches a crescendo at the low. The level of volume at the breakout point is not crucial. The fact that the price falls below the neckline is sufficient evidence that the tide has turned.

A minimum ultimate price objective is obtained by measuring the distance from the head to the neckline and projecting it down from the breakout point. Under this interpretation, the deeper the pattern, the greater its significance. Also bear in mind that the longer it takes to form the pattern, other things being equal, the greater its importance. A pattern that takes a few hours to develop on the intraday charts is obviously much less significant than a battle between buyers and sellers that takes several months.

In Figure 4-19 the neckline is horizontal, but head-and-shoulders formations can come in many shapes and forms. In Figure 4-20, we see an upward-sloping neckline, because this is an upward-sloping head and shoulders. The pattern is just as valid, since the head is still higher than the two shoulders. However, unlike a horizontal head and shoulders, which indicates a neckline violation and a reversal of the rising peaks and troughs simultaneously, the upward-sloping break occurs in two parts, with a neckline break first and a peak-and-trough break later. While the neckline violation is still valid, the sig-

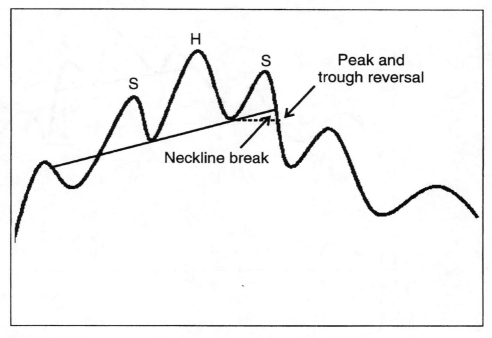

FIGURE 4-20.

nal is not so strong, since it represents only one piece of evidence that the trend has reversed.

Figure 4-21 shows a downward-sloping head and shoulders together with its measuring objective.

Head-and-shoulders formations are sometimes more complex, as shown in Figure 4-22. On the left we see a small head-and-shoulders top, which is actually the left shoulder of a much larger pattern. There is another small top on the right. Since these complex patterns reflect a much more involved battle between buyers and sellers, they are usually followed by a far more significant move when the breakout finally takes place.

REVERSE HEAD AND SHOULDERS

Head and shoulders also appear at the end of a downtrend (Figure 4-23), when they are known as inverse head and

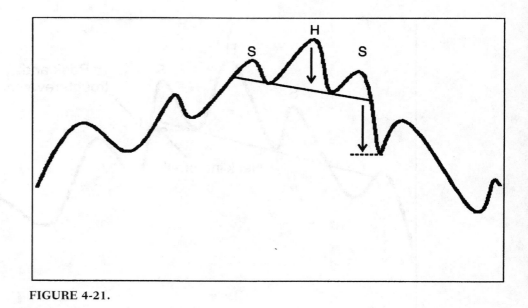

FIGURE 4-21.

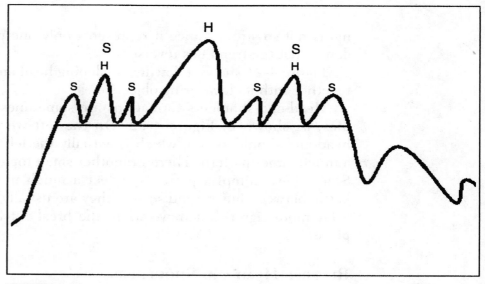

FIGURE 4-22.

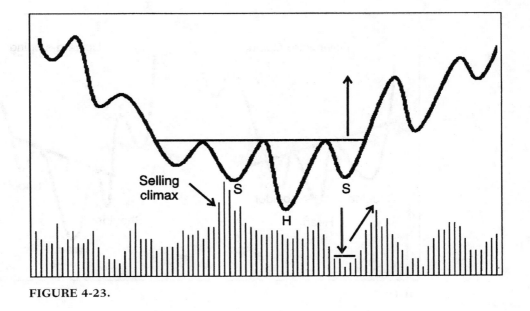

Selling climax

S

H

S

FIGURE 4-23.

shoulders or head-and-shoulders bottoms. Here we see the final low, the head, separated by two smaller declines, the left and right shoulders. Normally volume is lowest on the base of the right shoulder, but it is of paramount importance that volume expand on the right-shoulder rally, accelerating in activity as the breakout takes place. Sometimes the left shoulder or the head witnesses a huge increase in volume, known as a selling climax. It is not a prerequisite, but when a climax materializes it represents a valuable clue that the balance between supply and demand is in the process of reversing. Measuring objectives are calculated by projecting the distance between the head and the neckline at the point of the break-out.

Figure 4-24 shows that head-and-shoulders bottoms can occur as downward-sloping or upward-sloping, just as tops do.

CONTINUATION HEAD AND SHOULDERS

Head-and-shoulders patterns also occur as consolidation formations during a price trend. Figure 4-25 looks to be a top

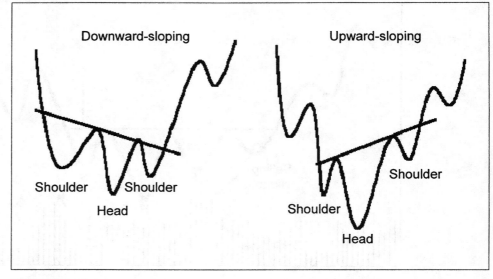

FIGURE 4-24.

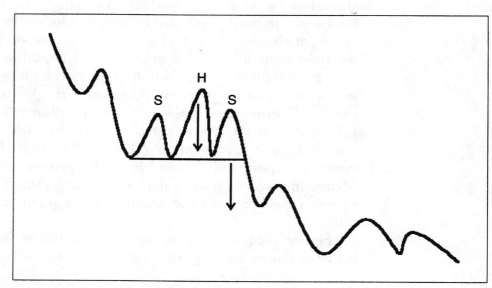

FIGURE 4-25.

formation during a downtrend—but it is really a consolidation. Note that the measuring principles are the same. Since a head-and-shoulders continuation formation in a downtrend occurs in a bear market, do not expect to see the huge volume on the head and right shoulder that you would in a reversal pattern of a market peak. Figure 4-26 shows a consolidation reverse head and shoulders during an uptrend. Note the expansion of volume on the breakout.

HEAD-AND-SHOULDERS FAILURES

Sometimes a head-and-shoulders pattern appears to be forming (Figure 4-27), but instead of breaking below the neckline, the price takes off on the upside. Alternatively, the neckline is violated (Figure 4-28), but the break turns out to be false. In either of these instances, the head and shoulders does not "work" and we are left with a false sense of weakness. Such situations are often, but not always, followed by explosive advances. This is probably because a substantial number of

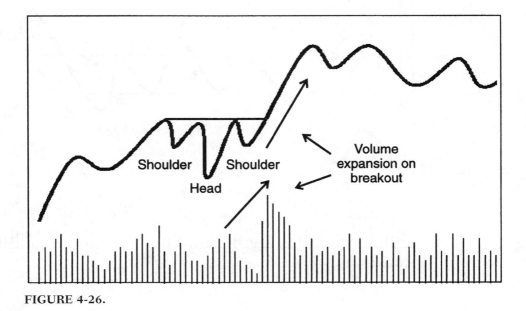

FIGURE 4-26.

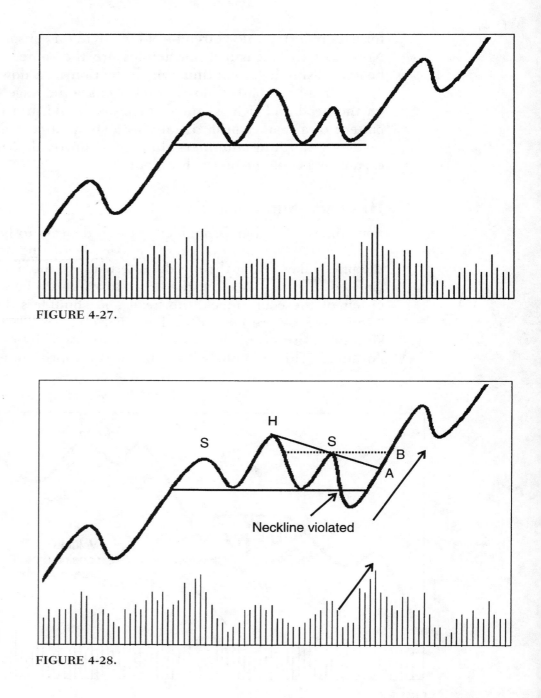

FIGURE 4-27.

FIGURE 4-28.

people put on short positions during the formation of the pattern, especially during the false breakdown. Later on, a few buyers are encouraged by the fundamentals and the shorts are forced to cover. Thus there becomes an urgency to buy, and prices move sharply higher. It is normal in such circumstances for volume to expand as the breakdown fails. It is often a good idea to have some kind of plan to decide ahead of time where to determine that the pattern has failed.

In this case, there are two possibilities in what I call the "1-2 rule:"

1. If the price violates the solid trendline, joining the head and the right shoulder, especially with expanding volume, it can be a signal of head-and-shoulders failure.

2. The level of the right shoulder can be used if the trendline joining the head with the right shoulder is particularly steep.

As we will learn later, steep trendlines are less reliable than those with a more shallow angle of ascent. If the price rallies above this shoulder zone, it often represents a timely signal that the pattern is not going to work. After all, the series of declining tops has now been reversed. Unfortunately, there is no way of knowing whether the failed pattern will be followed by a small or large rally. Sometimes prices explode, as in Figure 4-28. At other times, the market moves up to form another pattern just above the failed one. In any event, if you are short and have the least suspicion that a pattern is going to fail, it is best to get out of the way, for the pattern will likely be followed by a sharp rally or a confusing period of volatility.

Inverse head and shoulders also fail from time to time (Figure 4-29), and the same 1-2 rule applies to detecting these situations. The first line of defense lies in the area of the up trendline (A), joining the head with the right shoulder. The second is at the low of the right shoulder (B). Reverse head-and-shoulders formations that fail are often followed by an important decline, but the urgency of the selling is not usually

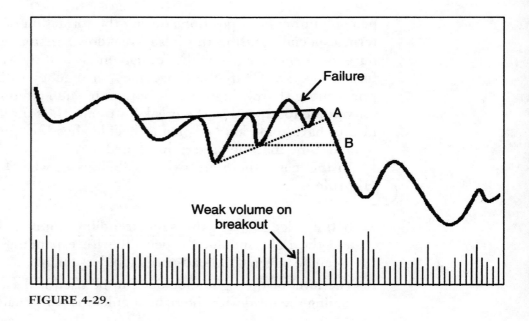

FIGURE 4-29.

as great as the need to buy following a head-and-shoulders top that does not work.

EXAMPLES

Now it is time to look at a few examples. Chart 4-7 shows a complex pattern for the Mexico Fund. I have marked the head and the two major shoulders, but there are also a couple of smaller shoulders (indicated by small letters). The battle between buyers and sellers is even more involved, because the top of the head is actually a rectangle formation. Note that volume is heaviest around the head and slightly lower on the right shoulder. Normally the contrast in the level of volume is much greater. As the price breaks below the neckline, there is a huge increase in the volume level, warning that a sharp decline is likely.

Chart 4-8 is another head-and-shoulders top. This one formed in Forest Labs at the time of the 1987 crash. See how

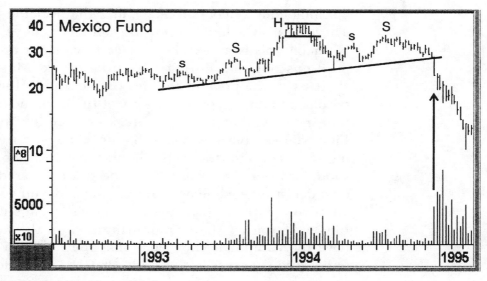

CHART 4-7. *Mexico Fund.*

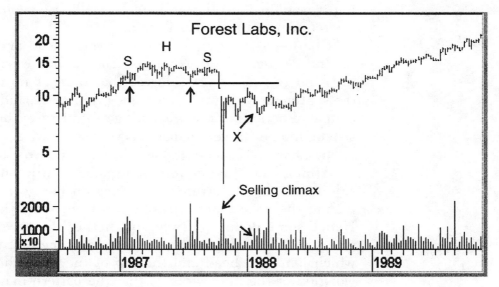

CHART 4-8. *Forest Labs, Inc.*

a selling climax occurs directly after the neckline penetration. There is also a low-volume retracement move at point X. Normally this is an excellent place to go short or to liquidate positions not sold during the initial break. Most people go short when the price penetrates the neckline. However, a better place to do it is in the vicinity of the neckline on a low-volume retracement move. There are three advantages here. First, you can place a stop at the neckline, at a trendline joining the head and the right shoulder, or just above the right shoulder itself. This will reduce the risk compared with a sale on a decisive neckline penetration. Second, you do not have to sit through the retracement rally with a losing position. Finally, if you go short around the area of the neckline, you have the additional knowledge that the rally is a low-volume one, which increases the odds that the breakdown will be valid. The disadvantage of waiting for the retracement move is that it may not take place! But remember there are lots of opportunities—there's always another train. In this particular instance, the low at the selling climax turned out to be the final low. However, at the time there was no sure way of knowing it was final, so the principle of selling or going short on the retracement move is still valid.

Chart 4-9 is an example of a reverse head and shoulders for the Portugal Fund. Note how the volume expands on the breakout to such a great degree that there is no doubt as to the sentiment of buyers. Sometimes volume expands for only a couple of periods as the breakout gets under way, but this consistent and pervasive expansion is very impressive.

In Chart 4-10, the right shoulder is somewhat anemic, but everything looks fine as volume expands a little on the downside breakout. Unfortunately, things do not go according to plan as the price again works its way back above the neckline. Hence some doubt arises as to whether the breakdown is a whipsaw. There are two lines of defense. The first is at line 1, which joins the head and the top of the right shoulder. Any violation of the line warns us that the pattern may indeed be failing. Since this is a pretty good trendline, anyone who is short would be advised to cover. The second line of defense is

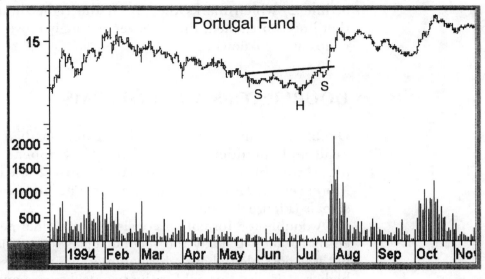

CHART 4-9.   *Portugal Fund.*

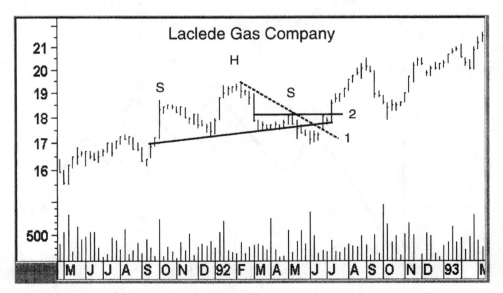

CHART 4-10.   *Laclede Gas Company.*

at line 2, which marks the top of the right shoulder. When that line is breached, the odds very strongly move in favor of a whipsaw breakdown.

DOUBLE TOPS AND BOTTOMS

Double tops and bottoms are less common than the various head-and-shoulders varieties, but they appear sufficiently often on the charts to be worthwhile looking out for. Moreover, when completed, they usually offer fairly reliable signals (Figure 4-30).

A double-top formation consists of two final peaks separated by a valley. Usually the second top is lower than the first, but it is possible to have a formation in which the second top is higher. It is also normal for the two peaks to occur at approximately the same level. The most important characteristic is that the second peak be associated with substantially less volume than the first. Volume at the second peak often shrinks to

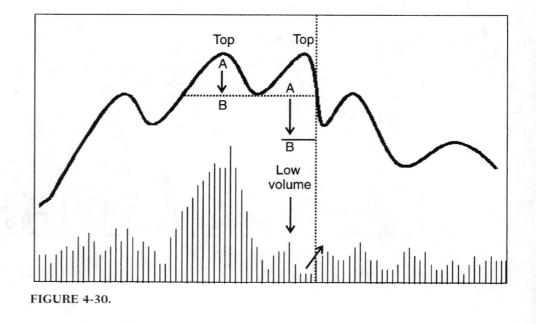

FIGURE 4-30.

almost nothing, indicating a complete disinterest. Since volume goes with the trend, this is a very abnormal situation and is therefore bearish. Volume also has a tendency to pick up after the second peak is formed, especially after prices have fallen below the valley line—the horizontal trendline separating the two tops. This too is abnormal, for in a healthy market volume declines with prices; it does not expand. Provided the second peak is associated with distinctly lower volume than the first one, it is not a prerequisite that it expand on the downside breakout. The fact that prices fall below the valley line is sufficient evidence. It is just that the expanding volume emphasizes the bearishness of the breakout.

The measuring objective (AB) is obtained by projecting the maximum distance from the higher of the two rallies down from the valley line. A double bottom (Figure 4-31) is a mirror image of a double top, with one exception: The breakout above the intervening rally high must be accompanied by expanding volume; otherwise the breakout is suspect. Again, it is very important to keep your eye out for a definite decline in volume at the second bottom. It doesn't matter if the price is

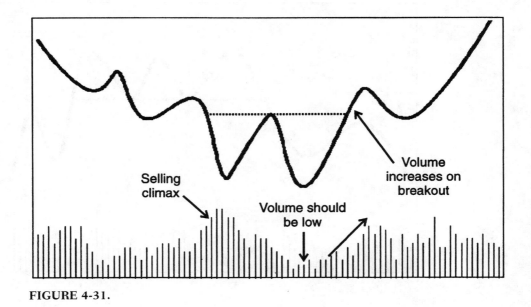

FIGURE 4-31.

slightly lower than the first bottom, though normally it is higher. The main point is that volume is distinctly lower. Quite often the first bottom is actually a selling climax, so the second one represents just a low-key test which turns out to be successful. Then, as the price rises, volume should expand slowly until the breakout point, when it should expand noticeably.

Double tops can also extend themselves to triple or even quadruple tops, though these are far less common than multiple bottom formations. Triple tops (Figure 4-32) tend to be more unstable affairs and do not always enjoy lower volume on the second or third peaks. The fact that they are extended versions of double tops means the battle between buyers and sellers is that much greater. Consequently, the ensuing bear trend has a tendency to be much more forceful.

Chart 4-11 shows a classic double top. The first top is associated with a high level of volume. The second one is not quite so high but is accompanied by a very much lower level of volume. When you see these characteristics, it is a good

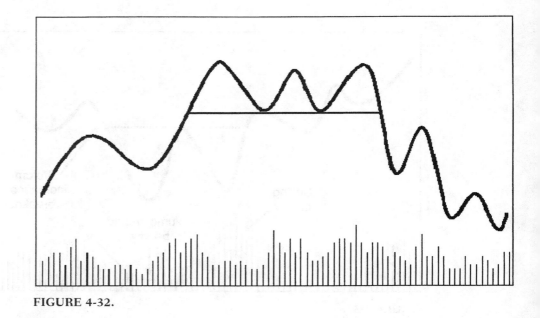

FIGURE 4-32.

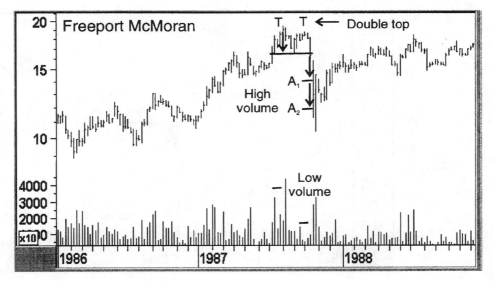

CHART 4-11. *Freeport McMoran.*

indication that the trend in question is about to reverse. The actual signal occurs when the price breaks below the valley separating the two tops.

Note that the price not only reached the downside objective (A1) almost immediately but went much further—more than twice the objective (A2). This was actually the final low for the move and normally we would expect to see a more lengthy decline follow such a formation. Even so, the size of the decline certainly met the downside criteria.

A classic double bottom is shown in Chart 4-12. Note how the first low is associated with a tremendous amount of volume—a selling climax, in fact. On the second low, trading activity is almost nonexistent. Also, note how volume declines on the rally following the selling climax. This almost guarantees a test of the first low. Then, as the price rallies from the second bottom, volume expands as it should.

The price then retreats and volume contracts, a typical retracement pattern. Finally, as the price breaks above the

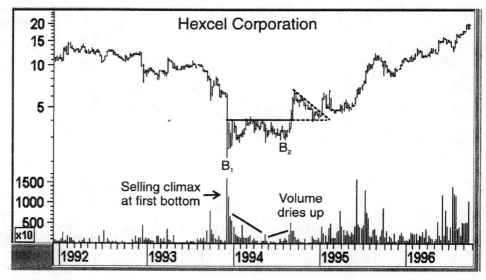

CHART 4-12.   *Hexcel Corporation.*

dashed retracement down trendline, volume starts to expand once again.

The final example, Chart 4-13, is somewhat unusual, since the first bottom is a spike. The second one ends as this slow, painful test manages to break above the dashed down trendline. The deliberate retracement under very quiet conditions is typical of the reaction to the second bottom. What is unusual is that the retracement begins almost as soon as the sharp rally ends. Normally we would expect the rally to end at about point X, and then to see a slow, steady decline materialize.

One final point is the fact that the price broke through the resistance valley line and subsequently found great support there during the frustrating consolidation phase.

BROADENING FORMATIONS

An orthodox broadening formation occurs when three or more price fluctuations widen out in size so that it is possible to construct two diverging lines joining the peaks and troughs (Figure 4-33). This type of pattern is quite rare and is normal-

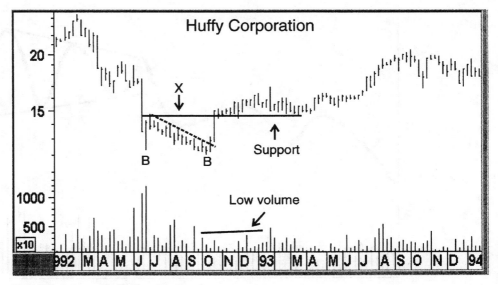

CHART 4-13. *Huffy Corporation.*

ly seen at market tops. The widening trading band indicates a
very unstable emotional situation. Consequently, when the
pattern is finally completed with a break in price below the
lower down trendline, a nasty decline often follows. An easier
type of broadening formation to spot is the right-angled variety
(Figure 4-34). At market peaks it is called a broadening formation with a flat bottom. It is constructed from two diverging
lines. The first joins a series of at least three rising peaks (line
AB), and the second is a horizontal line which halts at least
two reactions (line CD). When the price breaks below the flat
bottom, it usually signals that an unexpectedly sharp decline is
under way. Since the last rally is the final one in the bull
trend, volume is frequently heavy, so there is often no advance
warning of underlying technical weakness. Whenever you spot
a broadening formation with a flat bottom, my advice is to get
out of the way quickly, for the declines that follow are usually
much greater than you would expect from the size of the formation.

In effect, the formation in Figure 4-35 is a head-and-
shoulders top which is so bearish that there is not enough

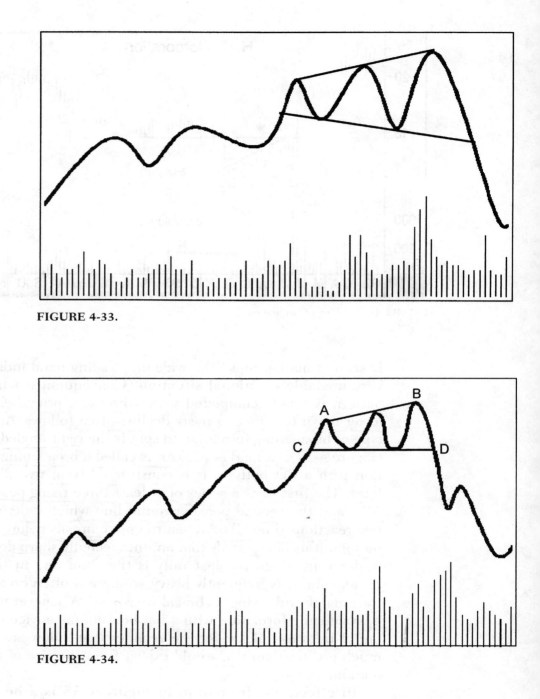

FIGURE 4-33.

FIGURE 4-34.

time to form the right shoulder. The dashed line represents the theoretical path of a left shoulder and downside breakout.

Right-angled broadening formations (Figure 4-36) also develop at bottoms, where they are known as broadening formations with flat tops. Here again, they are really head-and-shoulders bottoms in which the situation is so bullish that there is not enough time to wait for the formation of the right shoulder. The power of these formations was demonstrated at the beginning of the great 1980s bull market in equities in the United States. It was signaled in the summer of 1982 by the Dow completing such a pattern.

As with all upside breakouts, volume is key. It must expand on the breakout to indicate enthusiasm and therefore a change in the supply-and-demand balance in favor of demand. Another point worth noting is that the breakout rally should be an almost straight-line affair. Occasionally the price may pause for breath, and since this is a very dynamic pattern, the correction moves are usually pretty sharp, but well worth persevering with, because the overall move is normally very worthwhile.

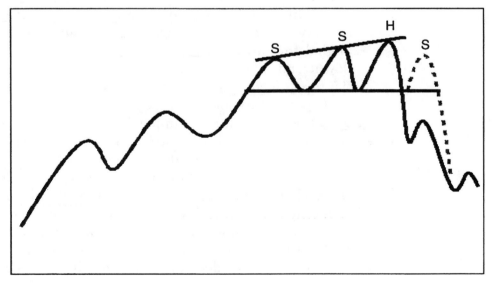

FIGURE 4-35.

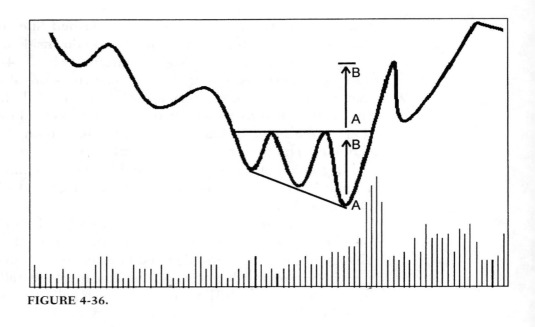

FIGURE 4-36.

Measuring objectives are obtained by calculating the maximum distance between the horizontal trendline and the price (AB) and projecting that distance from the breakout point.

Finally, right-angled broadening formations may be observed as continuation patterns. Figure 4-37 is a right-angled formation with a flat bottom as a continuation in a downtrend. Figure 4-38 shows a broadening formation with a flat top as a continuation in an uptrend.

Chart 4-14 shows a broadening formation with a flat bottom. It is not a classic example, because the rally peaks cannot easily be connected with a trendline. Also, a false break occurs at point X. These things do not matter too much. Just bear in mind that it is the spirit of the formation we should really consider. That is, the highest point is the final rally and the rallies generally are getting higher as the pattern develops. Finally, there is a rough horizontal area or zone of support which turns back all the reactions. Even though the patterns are usually followed by sharp declines, they are often subject to retracement moves.

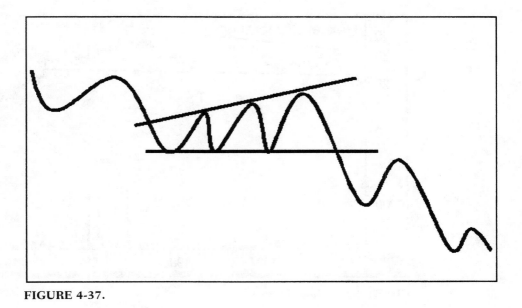

FIGURE 4-37.

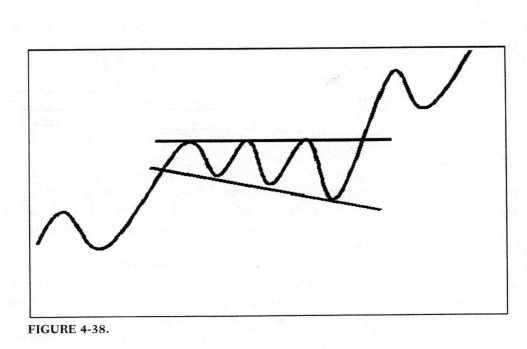

FIGURE 4-38.

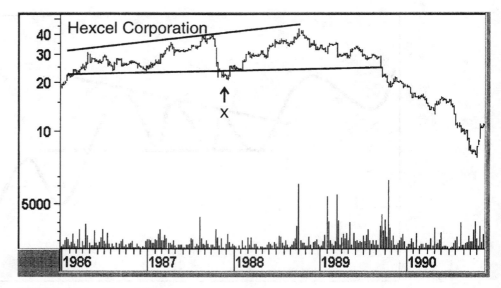

CHART 4-14. *Hexcel Corporation.*

In Chart 4-15 we again see that one of the rallies, at point X, was too small to enable its convenient connection to the trendline. However, there can be no mistaking the broadening aspect of the formation. Volume was almost nonexistent at the final high. This formation is somewhat different from the classic configuration because the flat bottom is rising. In a sense, it is a broadening channel, since each rally gets progressively stronger. In any event, breakdowns from these types of formations are normally reliable, though the ensuing declines do not appear to be as formidable as those which follow the flat-bottom variety. Finally, it is clear that the measuring objective (the distance between the peak and the flat bottom) was more than achieved.

Chart 4-16 is a case study showing a broadening formation with a flat top. We can also see a small retracement move at point X. Indeed, sometimes such corrective action takes the price back below the breakout line. This pattern is not a classic, since many of the rallies and reactions do not touch the two trendlines. Even so, it worked very well indeed, especially

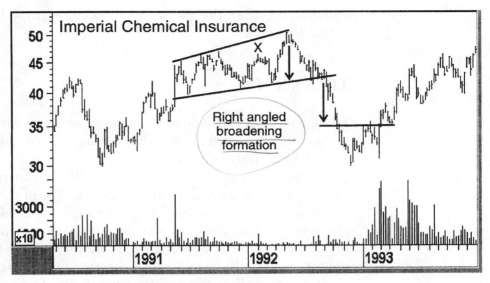

CHART 4-15. *Imperial Chemical Insurance.*

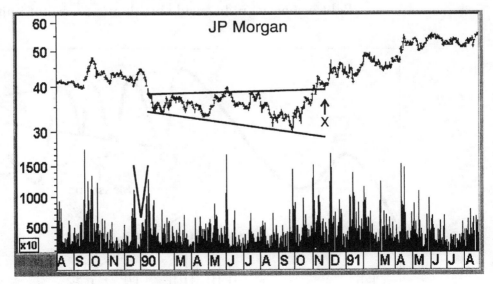

CHART 4-16. *J. P. Morgan.*

considering that the peak in volume developed before the actual breakout.

TRIANGLES

Triangles are a fairly common variety of price formation, but are notoriously unreliable. They come in two varieties: symmetrical and right-angled.

A symmetrical triangle (Figure 4-39) is constructed from two converging trendlines that join a series of *declining* tops and *rising* bottoms. Triangles are sometimes called coils, since the price fluctuations become progressively narrow and have the appearance of a coil that is being wound tighter and tighter, eventually springing out through one of the trendlines.

It is generally accepted that breakouts from triangles are more reliable when they occur about one-half to three-fourths of the distance between the beginning of the pattern (A) and the apex (B). It is normal for volume to shrink as the pattern forms, and to expand on upside breakouts. Volume can be light or heavy on downside breakouts—it is not important.

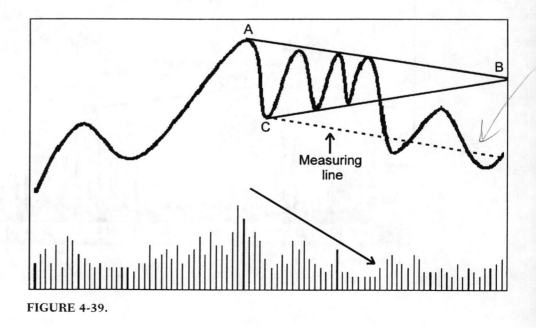

FIGURE 4-39.

Measuring procedures for symmetrical triangles are different from those for other patterns. For downside breakouts, it is first necessary to construct a measuring line parallel to the upper trendline. The parallel line begins at the first reaction low (C) and then becomes a dynamic measuring objective. Since the line is declining, the price takes longer to reach it, and the objective is lower. In my own experience I have not found this to be a particularly helpful approach, since more often than not the price easily exceeds the modest objective.

In Figure 4-40 upside objectives are achieved by constructing a line parallel to the lower, rising trendline and projecting it. Notice how the objective is exceeded, but the return move finds support at the extended measuring line.

Triangles appear in the charts as both reversal and continuation formations. Figure 4-41 shows the various possibilities. Note how the volume experiences a noticeable decline as each pattern is formed.

Right-angled triangles (Figure 4-42) are, in general, more reliable than their symmetrical counterparts. While both lines converge, as in the symmetrical variety, one of the lines in a

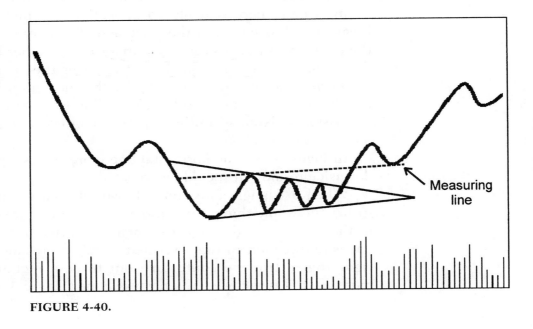

FIGURE 4-40.

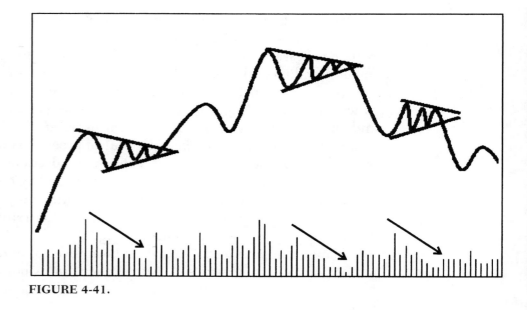

FIGURE 4-41.

right-angled formation is horizontal or at a right angle to the vertical (price) axis. Although we should assume that a symmetrical triangle will be resolved in the direction of the prevailing trend, there is really no indication of which way the breakout will occur until the price actually penetrates one of the lines. With the right-angled variety, on the other hand, we do get an indication from the direction of the slope of the nonhorizontal line. In this example, the indication is for an upside breakout, since the horizontal line represents an area of resistance. Note again the importance of expanding volume on an upside breakout.

In Figure 4-43, the horizontal line represents support, so a downside resolution should be expected.

When a triangle fails, one of two alternatives develops. Either the whole thing turns into a rectangle (Figure 4-44) or, in the case of a right-angled triangle, the price breaks in the opposite direction to that expected. A failed breakout from a right-angled triangle could turn out to be a rectangle, but more often it is followed by a nasty decline (Figure 4-45).

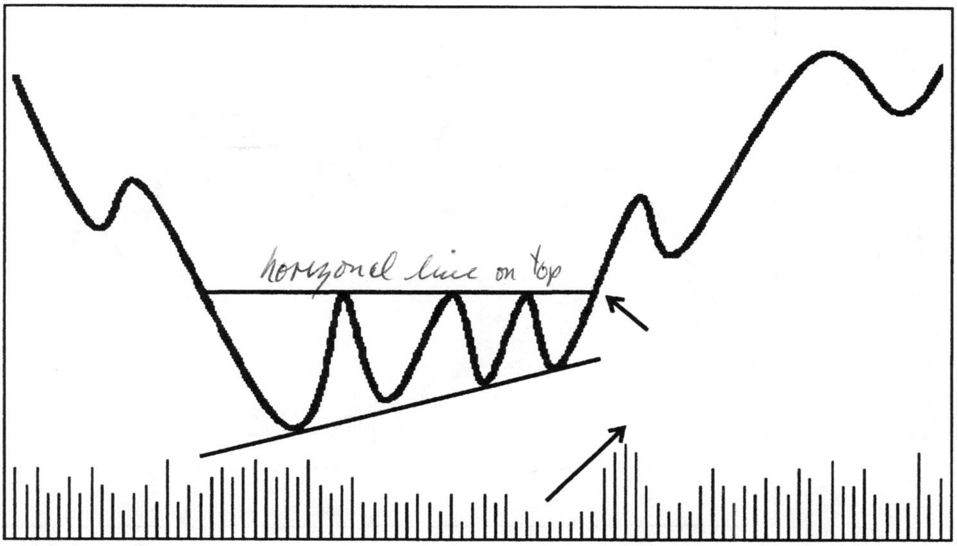

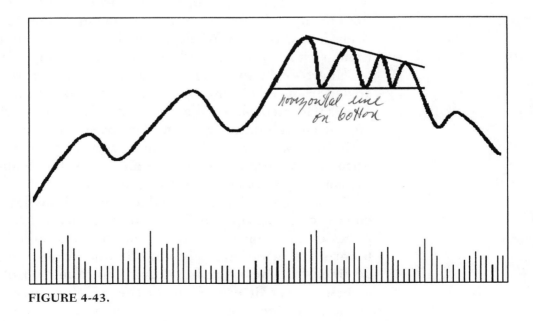

FIGURE 4-42.

FIGURE 4-43.

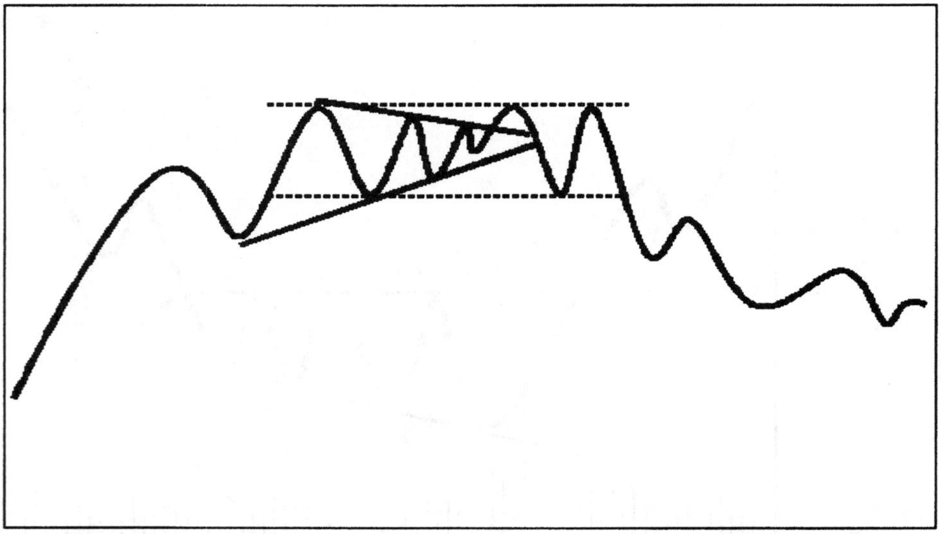

FIGURE 4-44.

Chart 4-17 shows a symmetrical triangle top. Note that the downside breakout develops roughly three-quarters of the way from the apex. Volume action is unusual in that it remains relatively heavy, but nevertheless remains in a slightly declining trend, so it is consistent with a symmetrical triangle formation.

Chart 4-18, showing the Korea Fund, features a right-angled triangle bottom. I have called it a bottom, but perhaps since it formed above the low it should be termed a right-angled consolidation pattern. The breakout was associated with an expansion in the volume level, but not much. The price gap is more impressive. In any event, the completion of the pattern was followed by an explosive advance.

It looked as if a right-angled ascending triangle was under construction in the stock shown in Chart 4-19. However, prices did not oblige, and the rising line was severely violated before the price could break out on the upside. Volume declined to almost nothing during the formation of the pattern; however, it expanded on the negative breakout. The ensuing decline looks severe, but, believe me, such triangle failures are often followed by similar weakness. All-in-all, a classic example of triangle failure.

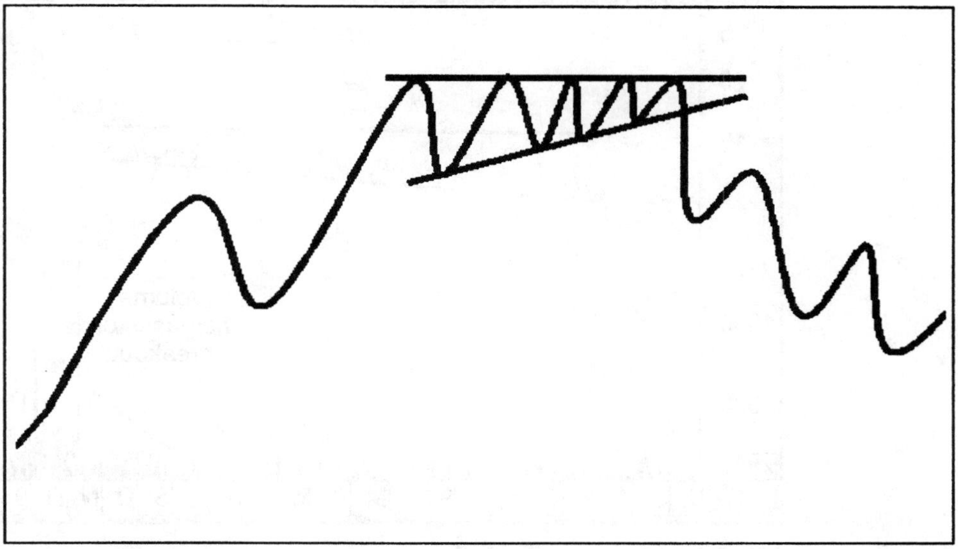

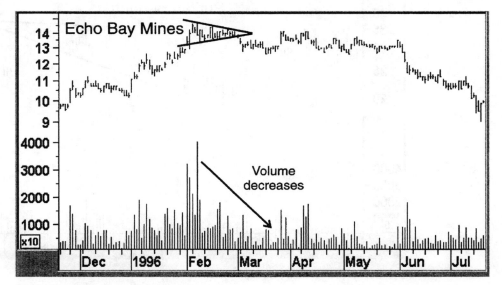

FIGURE 4-45.

CHART 4-17.   *Echo Bay Mines.*

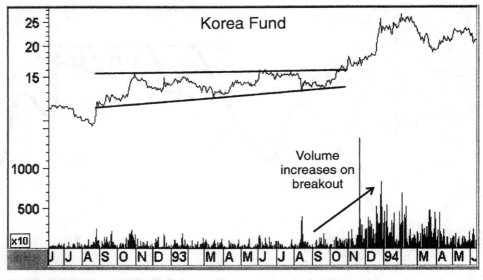

CHART 4-18. *Korea Fund.*

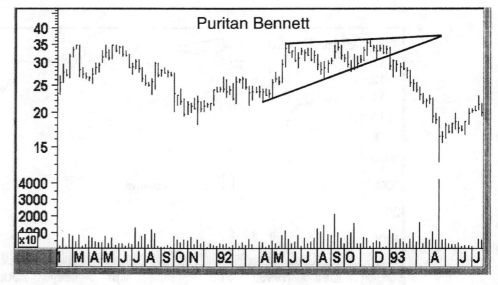

CHART 4-19. *Puritan Bennett.*

We will end this triangle section on a more optimistic note. Chart 4-20 shows a triangle that failed, but this time the price broke to the upside. The horizontal support zone, combined with the declining trendline joining the June and July peaks, had all the appearance of a declining right-angled triangle. However, it was worth waiting for the breakout before selling, because the decline simply didn't come. Instead, the breakout came on the upside with quite a vengeance. See how the volume expanded considerably on the breakout day.

SUMMARY

1. Rising and falling trends are not usually straight-up and straight-down affairs but are separated by transitional periods in which the psychological balance between buyers and sellers shifts. These transitional periods can often be spotted with clearly identifiable price patterns or formations.

2. Price patterns may also occur during an uptrend or downtrend, in which case they are consolidation or continuation

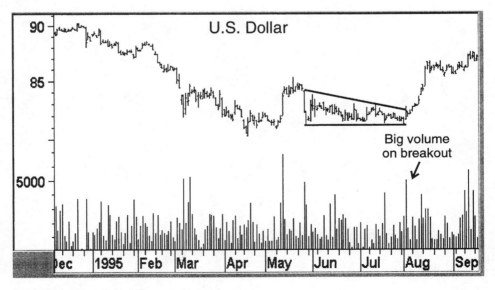

CHART 4-20.   *U.S. dollar.*

formations. Since a trend is assumed to be in force until evidence to the contrary appears, it is normal to expect the price pattern to be resolved in the direction of the prevailing trend (i.e., as a continuation rather than a reversal formation).

3. The importance of a price pattern is derived from its size and depth.

4. It is possible to ascertain measuring objectives for patterns. These are usually minimum targets and need not necessarily be achieved in one move.

5. Volume goes with the trend. It is of paramount importance to make sure volume expands on upside breakouts. Declining volume on rallies is bearish, as is expanding activity on declines.

6. Patterns which fail are often followed by powerful moves in the opposite direction to that indicated.

THE UPS AND DOWNS OF TRENDLINES

Trendlines are one of the most simple, yet effective tools of technical analysis. They are constructed by connecting a series of peaks or troughs (Figure 5-1). Down trendlines connect rally highs, or peaks. Up trendlines connect a series of bottoms.

Since markets also move in trading ranges, trendlines may be horizontal (Figure 5-2) as they connect the rally highs or bottoms that occur at the same level. The neckline of a head-and-shoulders pattern or the top and bottom of a rectangle formation are really trendlines.

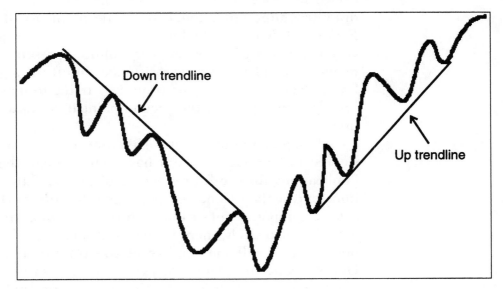

FIGURE 5-1.

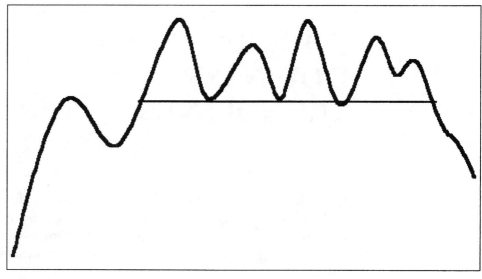

FIGURE 5-2.

In order to draw a proper trendline, it is first necessary to have two reversal points to connect; otherwise it is a line drawn in space with no technical significance. Often people draw trendlines that touch only one point, as illustrated in Figure 5-3. See how the line misses the second peak. This is a very important point, since a trendline represents a dynamic moving area of support or resistance. In effect, a good trendline reflects the underlying trend it is trying to monitor. If the line does not connect the second point it is not a true trendline.

As long as the price remains above it, the uptrend is considered to be intact. Once it has been violated, there are two implications for the future course of prices. Either the violation represents a trend reversal signal (Figure 5-4) or it indicates a temporary interruption in the prevailing trend (Figure 5-5). Unfortunately, there is no way of knowing which of these possibilities will materialize at the time of the violation. Occasionally, some clues are given, as shown in Figure 5-6. For example, if the price is in the process of completing a top, as in a head-and-shoulders formation, the implication is for a

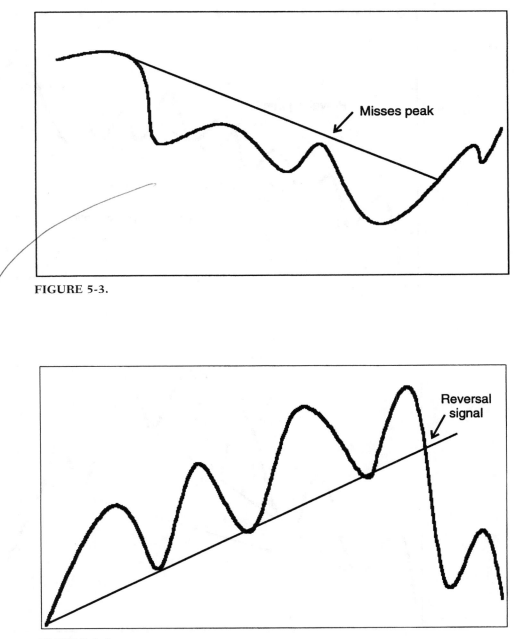

FIGURE 5-3.

FIGURE 5-4.

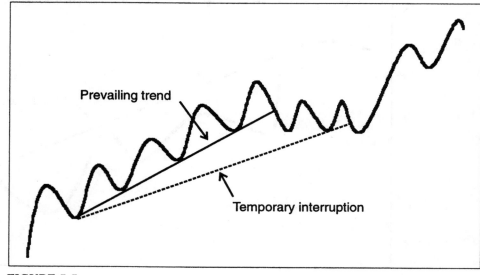

FIGURE 5-5.

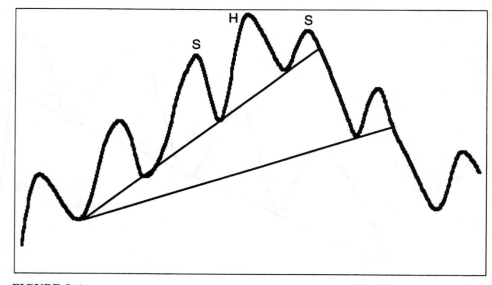

FIGURE 5-6.

signal of reversal. Figure 5-7 is another example of a trendline price pattern combination. Remembering our weight-of-the-evidence rule, we can now see that at the penetration of the line there are two pieces of evidence that the price trend has reversed the line, and the price pattern completion.

Figure 5-8 shows a similar phenomenon, this time featuring a reversal from a downtrend to an uptrend.

EXTENDED TRENDLINES

An often forgotten point concerning trendlines is the fact that once they have been penetrated, they reverse their roles as support and resistance. For example, in Figure 5-9 the up trendline represented significant support. Once it had been penetrated, it represented a barrier of resistance, as we can see from the fact that it turned back the final rally peak. Generally speaking, the greater the significance of a line as a support or resistance prior to its penetration, the greater its support or resistance role in reverse after the violation has

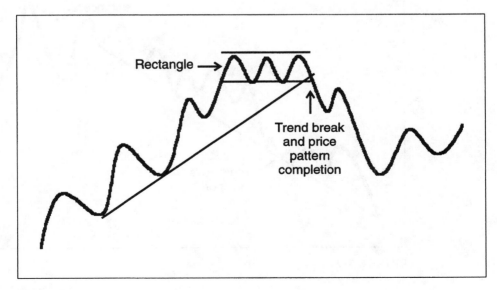

FIGURE 5-7.

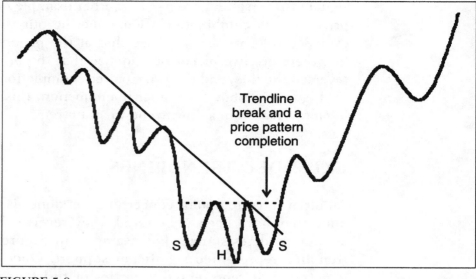

FIGURE 5-8.

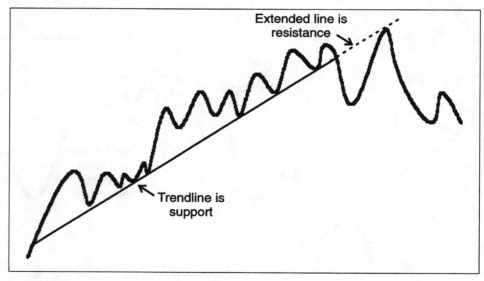

FIGURE 5-9.

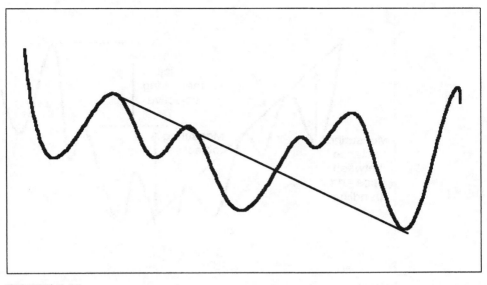

FIGURE 5-10.

taken place. Figure 5-10 shows the same situation, but this time from the aspect of a line reversing its role from resistance prior to penetration to support afterward.

Trendlines also offer measuring implications. Simply measure the maximum distance between the price and the trendline, as shown in Figure 5-11. In this case, it is the distance indicated by the arrow. Once the trendline has been violated, project this distance on the upside (measuring objective). Often prices will move in multiples of a price objective, which often serves as a pivotal support or resistance point (twice the measuring objective).

SIGNIFICANCE OF TRENDLINES

Trendlines obtain their significance from three factors: length, number of times touched or approached, and angle of ascent or descent. Let's consider each one in turn. The line in

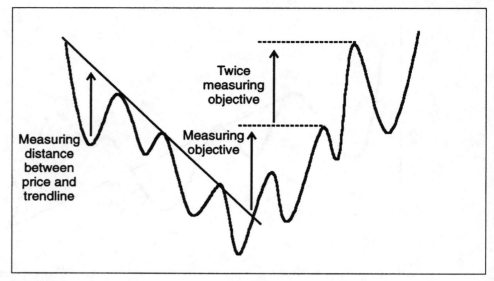

FIGURE 5-11.

Chart 5-1 is a relatively short one, and therefore monitors a short-term trend. A violation will have minor consequences. On the other hand, the line in Chart 5-2 is substantially longer and reflects a much greater trend. In this case, the time period between the high and low is about 12 years, meaning that a violation will have far more significant consequences.

Since a trendline reflects the underlying trend, it follows that the more times it has been touched or closely approached (Figure 5-12), the greater its significance as a support or resistance area (it better reflects the trend). I regard any line that has been touched or approached more than four times to be pretty significant. Of course, the degree of significance is influenced by the length of the line as well. Significance here also implies *reliability*, since trendline violations can often turn out to be whipsaws. Consequently, the more times a line has been touched or closely approached, generally speaking the more reliable the signal. Some people think that it is important only if the line is actually touched, but you may have noticed that I say "or closely approached." This is

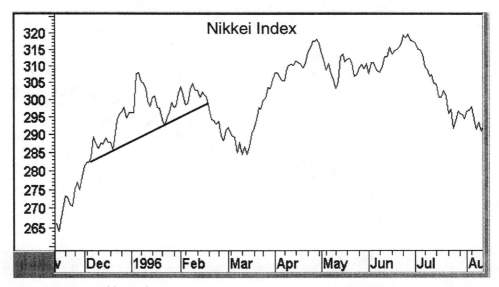

CHART 5-1. *Nikkei Index.*

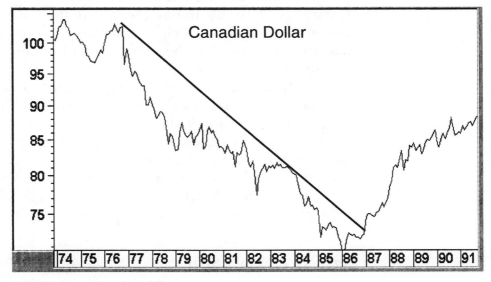

CHART 5-2. *Canadian dollar.*

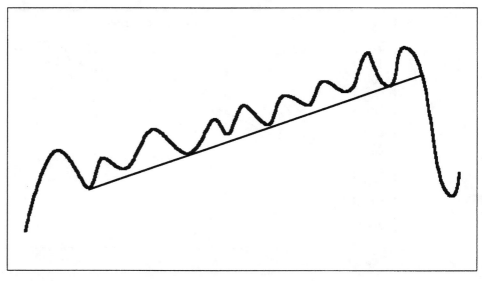

FIGURE 5-12.

because I look at a trendline as a dynamic zone of support or resistance. It is obviously cleaner if the line is touched. However, in my book a close approach, or even a temporary marginal violation, has the same effect of reinforcing the support or resistance concept.

The final point concerning significance arises from the steepness of the line itself. The very steep trendline in Figure 5-13 is clearly unsustainable. It is not, therefore, a very significant one. Often penetrations of steep lines are followed by consolidations rather than reversals, as is the case here. On the other hand, the line in Figure 5-14 is less steep and is more sustainable. Solely on the basis of angle of ascent, its penetration is likely to be that much more significant.

TREND CHANNELS

Occasionally, it is possible to construct a line that runs roughly parallel to the basic trendline (Figure 5-15). For example, if

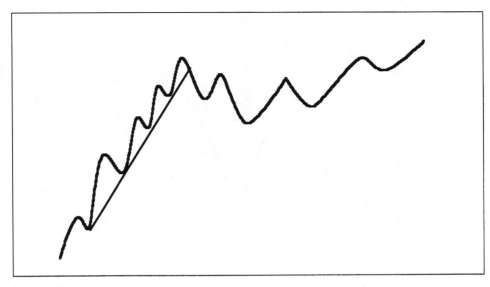

FIGURE 5-13.

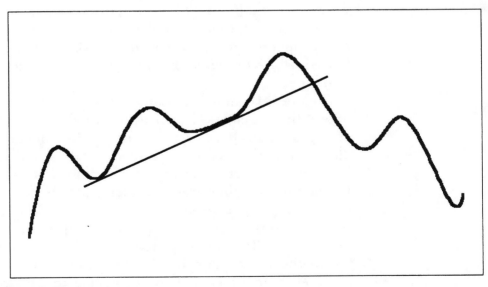

FIGURE 5-14.

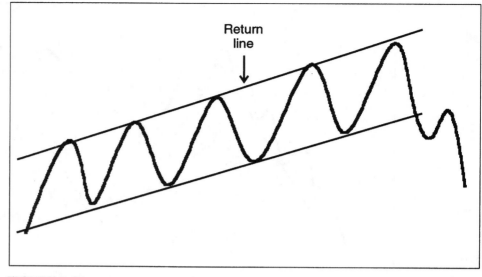

FIGURE 5-15.

we construct a line that joins a series of lows, we may be able to construct another joining the peaks. The lower line represents support, and the upper one, resistance. The top line is known as a *return line,* because it returns prices to the base trendline.

Figure 5-16 shows the same thing, but this time the return line is the lower one because the trend is down. Along with acting as a support or resistance point, depending on the direction of the trend, the return trendline has another use. When it is penetrated, one of two things is likely to occur. Either the prevailing trend accelerates or the move is temporary and represents exhaustion.

Let's consider the example of an uptrend, as shown in Figure 5-17. The line is penetrated at X; then prices accelerate to the upside and break completely out of the original channel. Sometimes it is even possible to construct another channel, with a steeper angle of ascent. This type of phenomenon often occurs after a price has broken out from a large

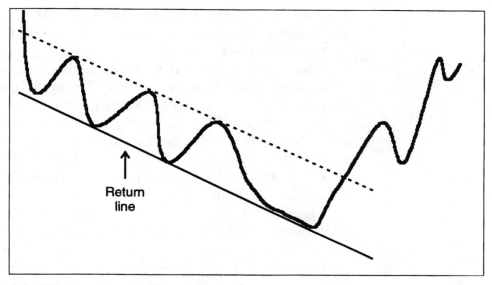

FIGURE 5-16.

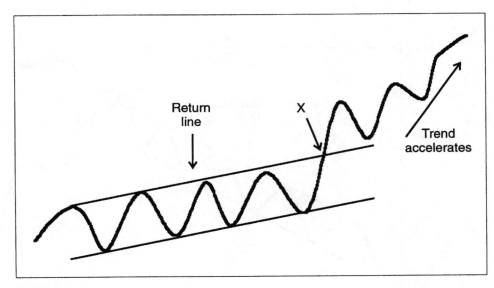

FIGURE 5-17.

base and has a fairly low angle of ascent. As people get more enthusiastic, they throw caution to the wind and bid up prices at a faster and faster pace.

The second alternative from a channel breakout, an exhaustion move, is not so positive (Figure 5-18). Exhaustion is more likely to occur after a fairly prolonged move. In this example, we see the price break above a steeper trend channel. Then, when more data is studied, we can see that the move ended in disaster. The price rallied on increasing volume, but was unable to hold its gains, eventually falling back below the return line.

Figure 5-19 shows the same two possibilities, this time for a declining trend. The question that needs to be answered is "How do you know which alternative will materialize?" Unfortunately, there is no clear-cut answer. Several factors need to be considered. How steep is the channel's angle of ascent or descent? The steeper the angle, the more likely an exhaustion move will develop. Does the breakout occur after

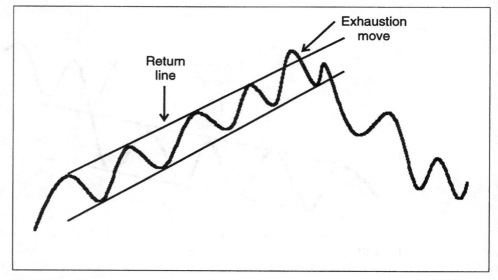

FIGURE 5-18.

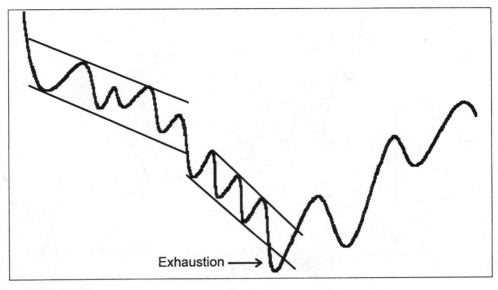

Exhaustion →

FIGURE 5-19.

the first wave of a primary trend, or is the trend fairly mature? If it is just breaking after the first wave, there is likely to be an acceleration breakout.

Another point to bear in mind is that a break which can sustain itself is more likely to be of the acceleration variety. In other words, the longer the price can remain outside the bounds of the channel, the lower the odds of an exhaustion move. By definition, an exhaustion move is a temporary, emotional phenomenon.

Sometimes it is not possible to construct a regular trendline because of price volatility, but it is possible to draw what would be a return line in a trend channel. In a rising market, this line would join a series of peaks. These lines, like return lines, serve the normal support or resistance role. However, it is also possible to use them in the same way as return lines, in that breakouts are followed either by an acceleration in the move or by an exhaustion. Figure 5-20 is an example during a downtrend.

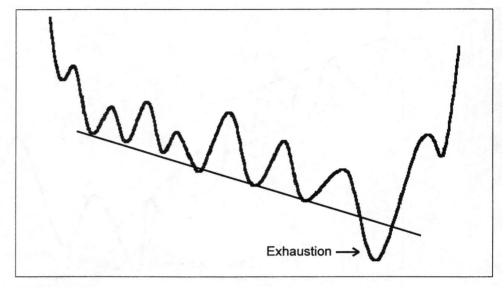

FIGURE 5-20.

CORRECTIVE FAN PRINCIPLE

The first rally in a bull market is often explosive, so the rate of ascent of the price advance is unsustainably steep (Figure 5-21). This often develops because the rally is a technical reaction to the previously overextended decline as speculators, caught short, rush to cover their positions. Consequently, any trendline drawn off the bottom is quickly violated (line A). The next line (line B), by definition, rises at a slower rate, but it too is eventually penetrated. The process is repeated for a third line (line C). This is known as the *fan principle,* and the lines, if drawn against intermediate lows, roughly correspond to the three stages of a bull market. The rule is that once the third line has been violated, the end of the bull market is confirmed.

The principle, as shown in Figure 5-22, is just as valid for down trendlines, and in this case has been applied to an intermediate trend movement. The lines join short-term turning

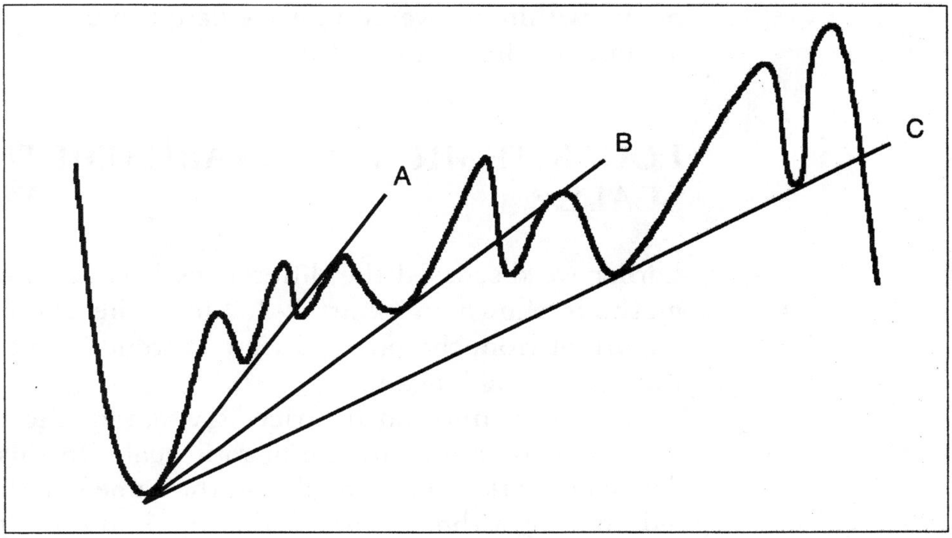

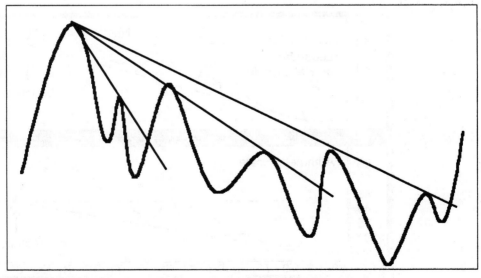

FIGURE 5-21.

FIGURE 5-22.

points within an overall intermediate trend, not an intermediate one within a primary trend.

LOGARITHMIC VERSUS ARITHMETIC SCALE

Earlier we discussed the differences between the two scaling methods shown in Chart 5-3. Since the choice of scale is important from the point of view of trendline penetration, it's worth covering it again.

When an uptrend in price is violated, the violation will occur first on a logarithmic or ratio scale. In this chart of the deutsche mark against the dollar, the same data has been plotted on a logarithmic scale at the top, and on arithmetic scale in the lower panel. Both lines connect the 1969 and 1971 lows. The violation on the ratio logarithmic chart occurs in December 1980, at 50. The arithmetic chart, on the other

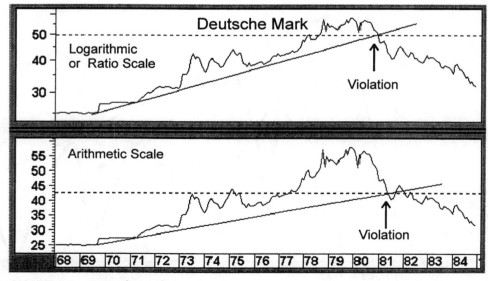

CHART 5-3. *Deutsche mark.*

hand, does not experience a violation until mid-1981, at 42. See how the logarithmic line at the top is touched or approached in 1972 and 1975, unlike the arithmetic one, so it is a far more significant line.

The same principle holds in reverse for downtrends (Chart 5-4). That is, arithmetic lines are the first to be penetrated, and then logarithmic (ratio) lines. In this chart of AAA U.S. bond yields, the logarithmic line is penetrated at the end of 1994, yet the arithmetic one is violated almost 5 years earlier, in 1990. Neither trendline is very reliable, but you can certainly see the difference between the two scales.

The examples I've used here are relatively long-term charts. For short-term charts, spanning 3 to 4 weeks, the price movements are relatively small, even for volatile price series. Consequently, it doesn't make much difference as to which scaling method is employed. However, since the logarithmic or ratio scale plots proportionately, and security prices reflect mass psychology, which tends to move in proportion, logarithmic is the preferred scaling method.

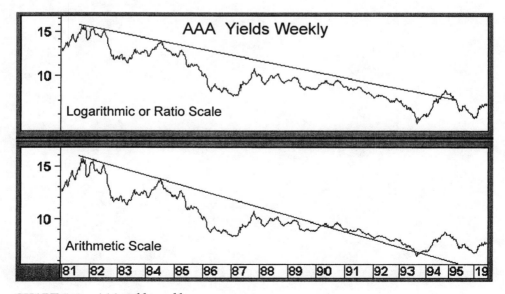

CHART 5-4. *AAA yields weekly.*

SUMMARY

1. Drawing trendlines can be something of an art. The main point to bear in mind is that a good trendline should reflect the underlying trend.

2. Trendlines represent dynamic areas of support and resistance.

3. The significance of a trendline comes from its length, the number of times it has been touched or approached, and the angle of ascent or descent.

4. Trendline violations are followed by either a reversal or a consolidation, after which the trend is resumed but at a less hectic pace.

5. When violated, extended trendlines reverse their previous role as support or resistance.

PRICE PATTERNS FOR TRADERS

In this chapter we will take a look at some price configurations that, for the most part, develop *during* a trend. These formations generally take far less time to complete than those discussed in Chapter Four. As a result, they are only of short-term significance.

FLAGS

Figure 6-1 shows a typical flag during a rising market. It is a small pattern which is confined within two parallel trendlines. It rarely takes longer than 3 weeks to develop and is noticeable by the fact that volume shrinks to almost nothing by the time the price is ready to break out.

In a rising market, flags typically form during sharp, almost vertical rallies and break out in an upward direction.

In a relative sense, volume is normally very heavy on the breakout. A flag represents a period of very controlled profit taking, and the two parallel lines usually have a slight downward slope. There are no measuring implications, except for an old Wall Street saying: "Flags normally fly at half mast." In other words, if the rally is the flagpole, then the flag will often form halfway up the flagpole, or at the halfway point of the rally.

A good measuring procedure is to calculate the vertical distance between the rally low and the lower part of the flag, and then to project that distance up from the breakout point.

Figure 6-1 also shows a flag during a down market. The characteristics are more or less the same as bull market flags, except that the flag usually slopes in a contratrend direction

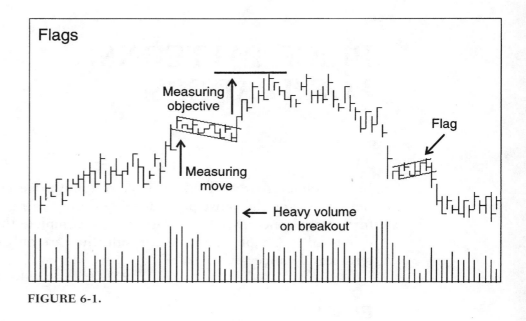

Flags

Measuring
objective

Measuring
move

Heavy volume
on breakout

Flag

FIGURE 6-1.

(i.e., up). Volume still shrinks with the formation of the pattern, but it is almost always the case that it expands considerably on the downside breakout. In effect, volume shrinks on the rally and expands on the decline, both of which are abnormal and therefore bearish characteristics. Flags in a bear market also have a tendency to fly at half mast.

If volume does not contract during the formation of what you think is a flag, watch out! If the flag takes longer than 4 weeks to develop, that is not a good sign. Remember flags are a controlled period of profit taking or loss consolidation in declining markets. Heavy volume and/or a lengthy forming period is not representative of that.

PENNANTS

If flags can be thought of as small rectangles, pennants are like triangles. In Figure 6-2, the pennant is constructed, not from two parallel trendlines, but from two converging trendlines, as with triangles.

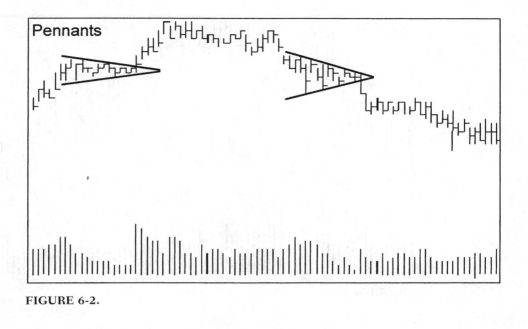

FIGURE 6-2.

All the other characteristics are the same as flags, except that volume usually decreases even more as the pattern progresses. This is probably because the price fluctuations are more subdued at the apex of a pennant than on the right side of a flag. The important thing to remember is that a pennant has converging trendlines, one of which is rising and one of which is declining.

Since pennants, like flags, rarely take more than 3 weeks to complete, they do not appear on the weekly and monthly charts, but are confined to daily and intraday charts instead.

WEDGES

Wedges, like pennants, are a form of triangles. The difference is that wedges are constructed from two converging lines that

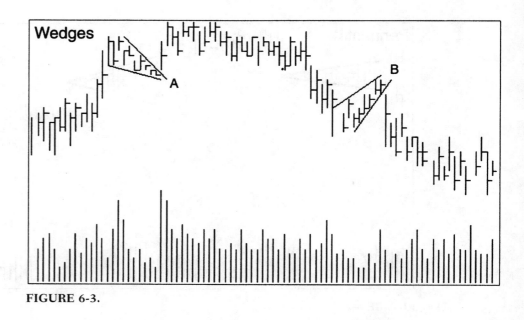

FIGURE 6-3.

are moving in the same direction (Figure 6-3). Pennants, on the other hand, are constructed from two converging trendlines that are sloping in different directions.

All other characteristics are similar. Since wedges are countercyclical patterns, they decline along with falling volume during uptrends (A). On the other hand, they rise with falling volume during declining trends (B). Rising wedges are fairly common as bear market rallies. Prices often slip precipitously on expanding volume as the price breaks out of the pattern on the downside.

SAUCERS AND ROUNDING TOPS

Saucer and rounding-top formations are rather rare in modern-day charts. A saucer is a circular price bottom (Figure 6-4) accompanied by a similar type of pattern in volume. The idea is that prices and volume gradually accelerate to the upside once the quiet, inactive bottom has been completed.

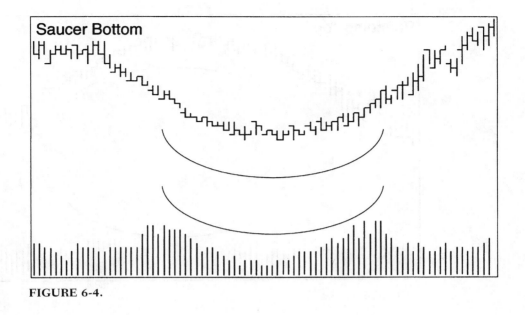

FIGURE 6-4.

Rounding tops (Figure 6-5) are the mirror image of saucers (rounding bottoms) so far as price is concerned, and the volume configuration is exactly the same. In this case, though, the rising volume at the end of the pattern is bearish because it is associated with declining prices. In a sense, the volume and price configurations form a kind of circle.

Unfortunately, because of the nature of these patterns, there are no obvious points that can be used for breakout purposes. Fortunately, since they do not appear on the charts too often, we are generally saved from the difficult task of having to decide when such formations have been completed.

KEY REVERSAL DAYS

A key reversal day occurs after a long move lasting many days or several weeks. The key reversal day is, in effect, a 1-day price pattern that separates what are normally two sharp price moves. In Figure 6-6, the day is a top formation. It is really an

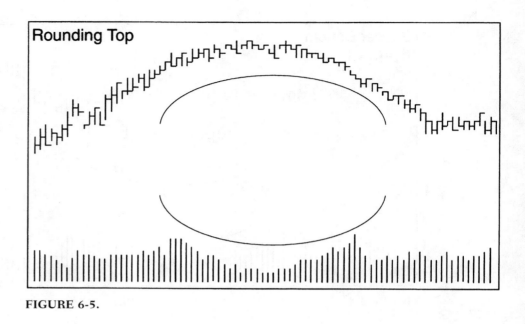

FIGURE 6-5.

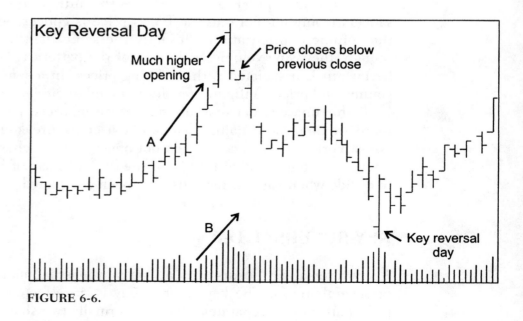

FIGURE 6-6.

exhaustion move, since it occurs after a huge run-up in both price and volume.

On a key reversal day, the price often opens up much higher than the previous day's high. Incidentally, the left tick reflecting the opening prices will be displayed in the rest of the diagrams in this section. The price may move higher in the early going, but by the end of the trading session the price closes below the previous close. Volume during this particular day is extremely heavy and marks the crescendo of the trend of rising volume that accompanied the price run-up.

For the day to qualify as a key reversal three conditions are necessary. First, it must be preceded by a sharp, almost exponential run-up, or decline in price (A). Second, volume should experience a parabolic run-up (B). Finally, prices should open up and move sharply in the direction of the previous trend, but close in the opposite direction to the way they opened—that is, down in a bull reversal and up in a bear reversal. While it is possible to have a reversal day in which the price does not close in the opposite direction, it is not a "key" reversal. In other words, in technical analysis we are working in probabilities. If the price closes in the same direction as the previous trend, it doesn't preclude a reversal; if it does, a reversal is that much more likely.

Since key reversals are short-term affairs, their effects are usually short term in nature. With that said, it is amazing how often such phenomena occur at turning points in intermediate and primary trends. In such cases, these exhaustion moves are the short-term dominoes which topple through to longer-term trend reversals. Key reversals usually occur on the daily charts, but they can be seen on weekly ones as well. In these cases, other things being equal, they will have greater importance as trend reversal agents.

2-DAY REVERSALS

Another short-term reversal phenomenon is the 2-day reversal (Figure 6-7). This one occurs after an important advance. On

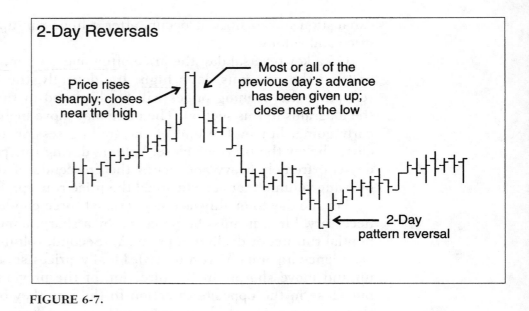

FIGURE 6-7.

the first day of the pattern, the price moves to a significant new high and closes at or near this high. On the second day it opens at around the same level, but by the end of the session it has retraced the entire advance of the previous day. The second day's closing occurs near or below that of the first day. It really helps to spot these 2-day reversals if volume is exceptionally heavy on both days. The psychology behind them is that traders come into the second day expecting the strong trend of the previous session to continue. However, confidence is shaken when prices not only don't go up, but instead go down.

Figure 6-7 also shows a 2-day reversal at a bottom. Remember, these formations, in and of themselves, have only short-term implications. However, since they reflect psychological exhaustion, the short-term top or bottom they are signaling often turns out to be associated with an intermediate reversal as well.

OUTSIDE DAYS

Outside days are quite common in daily charts (Figure 6-8), especially in the futures markets. They occur after a rally or reaction has taken place and are days in which the trading range is greater on both the upside and downside than the previous day. It is important for the close to occur in the opposite direction of the previous trend. For example, outside day A in Figure 6-8 not only surpasses the trading range of the previous day, but closes in the opposite direction (i.e., down). Outside day B, on the other hand, signals a reversal of a short-term rally.

It is important to note that outside patterns have only a short-term effect, sometimes as brief as 1 or 2 days, and rarely longer than 10. However, if you are a highly leveraged trader, they can provide excellent entry and exit points.

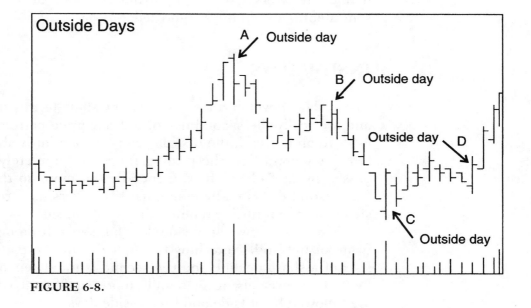

FIGURE 6-8.

Generally speaking, the more dramatic the outside day, the stronger the signal. Outside day C occurred after a relatively sharp decline and the outside day was quite exciting. In effect what we are seeing here is a dramatic shift of sentiment on the outside day. The sellers predominate at the beginning of the day, but by the end of the trading session they become exhausted as the buyers take over the driving seat.

Another strong outside day signal is shown in outside day D, where the range is greater than the three previous ones combined.

In all these examples, the close occurred in the opposite direction to the previous trend. Even if it occurs in the same direction, it is still possible for the outside day to be a signal of reversal, but obviously the odds are that much greater if the close occurs in the opposite direction. Don't forget the technical adage that there must be something to reverse. In other words, since the outside day reflects a change of market sentiment during the course of the trading session, there must be a previous trend in sentiment in order for a reversal to occur. Volume does not always expand on an outside day, but again if it does, it offers strong supporting evidence of a change in sentiment between buyers and sellers.

INSIDE DAYS

Inside days develop after a persistent short-term price move and are really the second day of a 2-day price pattern (Figure 6-9). In an uptrend, the first day consists of a fairly sharp rally. On the second day, the trading range is completely encompassed by that of the first. Generally the more so the better. The second day is really telling us that buyers have run out of steam, and that upside momentum is exhausted.

Figure 6-9 shows an inside day that separates a downtrend from an uptrend. Note how the first day of the pattern consists of a sharp decline and the second is totally encompassed by it. Key reversals are generally more significant when they are followed by outside and then inside days.

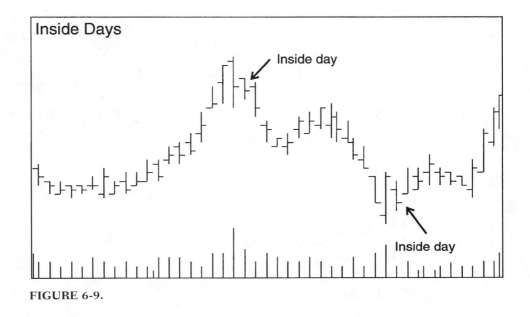

FIGURE 6-9.

GAPS

A gap occurs on a bar chart when the trading range of the current period falls completely above or below that of the preceding period. The gap then appears as an empty vertical space between two trading periods (Figure 6-10). Gaps typically reflect the highly charged emotional feelings of the crowd. For example, if a gap appears on the upside (gap A), it is telling us that the buyers are so motivated they are prepared to pay more for a security today than they did throughout yesterday's trading session.

Downside gaps (gap B) let us know that sellers are so fearful they are willing to liquidate at prices well below yesterday's trading range. Emotions in markets not only move to minor extremes such as this, but also swing back and forth like a pendulum. It is not surprising, therefore, that *most* gaps on the charts are sooner or later filled as the bullish or bearish extreme that caused them moves back the other way to a bearish or bullish extreme. An upside gap is said to be closed when

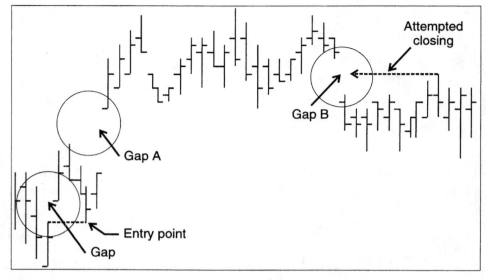

FIGURE 6-10.

the price bar of a subsequent day comes down sufficiently to cover all or part of the vacuum or blank space created on the way up. Sometimes the gap is not closed, but a good-faith effort is made to try to close it, rather like the *attempted closing* in Figure 6-10. There is an old saying that "the market abhors a vacuum"; and the closing, or attempted closing, of the gap is a way of accomplishing this.

Many traders like to enter the market at a point close to the lower part of the gap in an up market and close to the start of the gap in a down market (the *entry point* in Figure 6-10). Such positioning is often low risk because you soon find out whether you are right or not. If you are wrong, the market will tell you by moving quickly beyond the gap area.

By the same token, since most gaps are eventually filled, the odds of a successful trade are reduced if a position is taken shortly after an unfilled gap appears in the charts. I do not mean to imply that *all* gaps are filled—indeed, they are not—but most are. Gaps can mean different things in different markets. With the advent of 24-hour trading, many more gaps appear on the futures charts than was previously the case. Generally, a market will have few gaps, or those gaps will be closed if it is an active region for that particular security. For example, the mark is traded in several time zones, but as you can see in Chart 6-1, which reflects NYSE trading, the various sessions are fairly active. Consequently, gaps usually end up being filled. The major market for Japanese government bonds is the day session in Japan—so there are relatively few gaps. On the other hand, the bonds are also traded on the LIFFE exchange in London (Chart 6-2). Since this session accounts for much less volume, gaps are not nearly as important, and are far less likely to get filled.

The same comment can be made for thinly traded stocks versus highly liquid blue chips. Gaps in the former are not generally as significant as those experienced in NYSE blue-chip trading.

There are several types of gaps: breakaway, running, exhaustion, and common or area gaps. The last category is the least emotional and therefore least significant. Area gaps occur within a trading range, usually a price pattern such as a

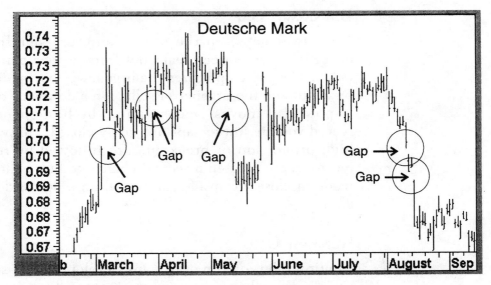

CHART 6-1. *Deutsche mark.*

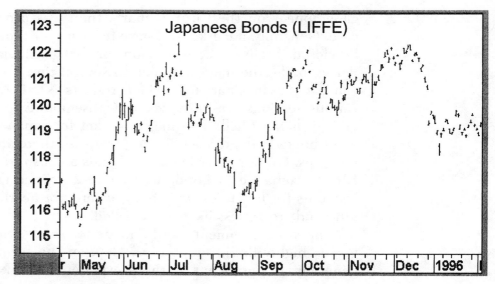

CHART 6-2. *Japanese bonds (LIFFE).*

rectangle. Gaps which develop as a result of stock going ex-dividend are also technically insignificant.

BREAKAWAY GAP

Breakaway gaps, on the other hand, are significant. They occur when the price breaks out from a price pattern (Figure 6-11). The gap emphasizes the urgency of buying in an upside breakout and the urgency of selling in a downside one. In really powerful moves, accompanied by humongous or even record volume, these gaps are rarely closed. However, since a high proportion of breakouts are followed by retracement moves, there is often a second chance to buy as an attempt is made to close an upside gap or sell on a downside gap-filling effort.

RUNAWAY GAP

Continuation, or runaway, gaps develop during straight-line price moves when prices are moving rapidly and emotions are

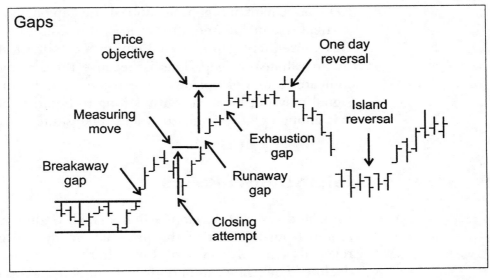

FIGURE 6-11.

running high. Because of this, if they are not closed in a day or two, they tend to remain "open" until the next intermediate swing in the opposite direction gets under way. Runaways are sometimes called measuring gaps, because they often occur halfway between the previous breakout and the ultimate termination of the move. Both the measuring move and the price objective are shown in Figure 6-11.

EXHAUSTION GAPS

Exhaustion gaps develop at the end of a move (Figure 6-11). They are usually preceded by at least one runaway gap. Volume is usually pretty heavy and prices then end their vertical rise and consolidate. An exhaustion gap is usually quite significant, since it can mark the termination of an intermediate trend. In Figure 6-11, the gap preceded a consolidation. Unfortunately, there is no real way to determine whether a gap is of the continuation or exhaustion variety until well after the fact. Two clues are useful. First, if the gap is the third or fourth in a series of continuation gaps, it is likely to turn out to be an exhaustion gap. Second, if the gap occurs after a near vertical rise or fall and after at least one continuation gap and this subsequent gap is closed within a day or so, it is likely to be an exhaustion gap. This is because the closing of the gap indicates a loss of upside or downside momentum. While this signal may not be sufficiently strong to liquidate the position, it is enough of a warning to at least take some profits.

ISLAND REVERSALS

An island reversal develops when a small trading range is separated from the rest of the price action by two gaps. Island reversals typically develop after a fairly persistent advance or decline. The island, in and of itself, only has short-term implications. However, when the reversals occur at the end of intermediate moves, as they often do, their importance is much greater. Quite often the island will represent a hat for the head of a head-and-shoulders formation. An example of an island reversal is shown in Figure 6-11.

One important type of reversal occurs when the bar for the trading session falls beyond not only the trading range of the preceding day, but that of the subsequent one as well. In effect, the price bar becomes an island separated from the rest of the price activity by the two gaps. For this reason, such phenomena are known as 1-day island reversals. It is also possible to get 1-week island reversals, but they are far less common.

EXAMPLES

Chart 6-3 features several examples of flags. Example A runs countercyclical to the uptrend, while B and C represent small rallies in a bear market. Note that both price movements are confined within two parallel lines. The October 1994 wedge is also a countercyclical rally, but the two trendlines marking the outer boundaries converge. Volume also shrinks a little as the wedge is formed. Normally we would expect to see volume dry up to an even greater extent as these consolidation formations develop.

Chart 6-4 offers an excellent example of an outside day. It occurred after a very sharp run-up in Newmont gold shares in early 1996. Since outside days developed in pretty well all of the gold shares, the pattern emphasizes the bearishness of the situation. This day was also associated with a substantial amount of volume, again emphasizing the very significant change in sentiment that took place.

Chart 6-5 features outside days that developed after a decline. The December 1995 outside day preceded a major rally in the silver price. Remember, an outside day is normally a short-term phenomenon, but in this case the day was followed by a very strong rally. The one that developed in early June 1996 did not work out so well. It was followed by a few days of strength, but later on the price actually made a new low. Its bullish effect was canceled out by another outside day that developed late in the month.

Chart 6-6 illustrates a 2-day reversal. See how the price runs up and closes at its high. The next day, prices open at the high and promptly proceed to decline throughout the session,

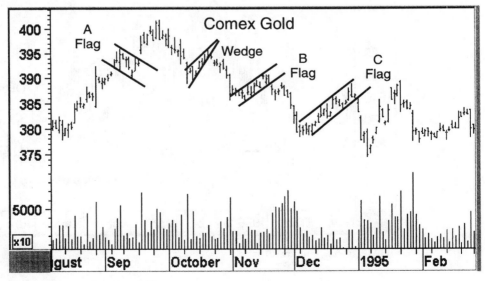

CHART 6-3. *Comex gold.*

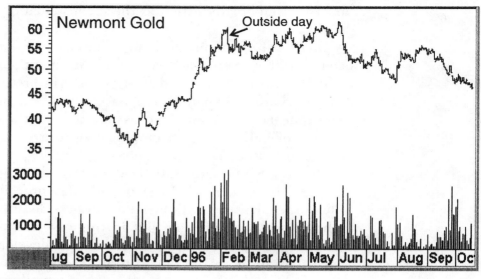

CHART 6-4. *Newmont gold.*

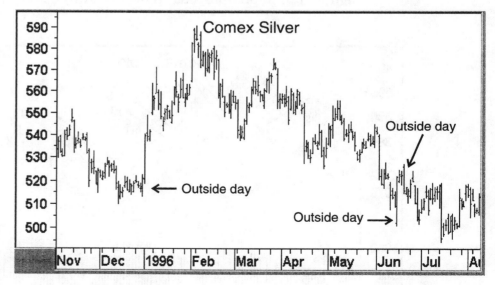

CHART 6-5. *Comex silver.*

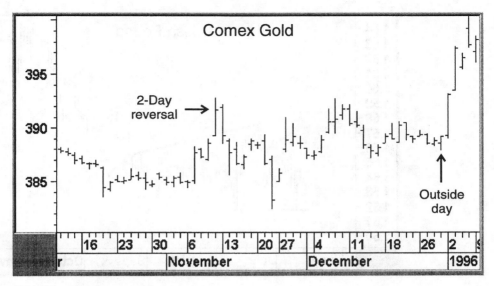

CHART 6-6. *Comex gold.*

finally closing close to the low. These 2-day price patterns often mark the emotional top to a short-term move. Even so, it's remarkable how often they can signal a more substantial market turning point.

Chart 6-7 shows some gaps in the British pound. The one in July was a bit of a breakaway gap as it jumped through a small trendline. Another developed in September. The first one was quickly filled later on in July, but it took several months before the second one filled. The runaway gap that developed in October was filled relatively quickly.

Also note the huge outside day that signaled the end of the rally in October. It encompassed not only the previous day's trading range, but the previous 10 days' as well.

SUMMARY

1. Flags, pennants, and wedges are almost always continuation patterns. Volume decreases considerably during their formation, which rarely takes more than 3 weeks and is often substantially less.

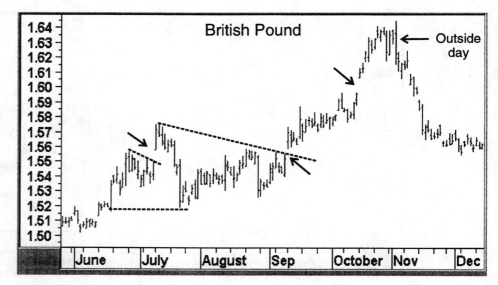

CHART 6-7.   *British pound.*

2. Flags have parallel lines like rectangles; pennants have two differing converging lines like triangles. Wedges are constructed from two converging lines that are moving in the same direction.

3. All three patterns normally occur during vertical price moves, both up and down.

4. Rounding tops and saucer formations are often followed by substantial price movements and reflect a gradual shift in the supply-and-demand balance. In both instances, volume contracts in the center of the pattern and expands at the two extremities.

5. A key reversal day is an exhaustion phenomenon. It has three principal characteristics. It should be preceded by a parabolic move in volume and price. The price should open strongly in the direction of the preceding trend. Finally, it should close in the opposite direction.

MOVING AVERAGES

THE CONCEPT

A quick glance at any chart representing market data shows that prices can be very volatile, almost haphazard at some point. Moving averages are probably the most widely used method of identifying trend reversals, since they do a good job of smoothing out these random fluctuations so that traders and investors can get a clear grasp of the underlying trend. As we shall see, moving averages are far from perfect, but are nevertheless an invaluable part of the technician's arsenal.

A moving average is constructed by smoothing the price data. There are various techniques for doing this, but for the most part they fall into two categories. One approach gives an equal weighting to each piece of data. That would be each day for a daily chart, each week for weekly charts, and so forth. The other broad technique seeks to give a greater weight to the more recent data, thus making the average more sensitive to price changes. In this presentation we will consider one of each type—namely, a simple and an exponential moving average.

SIMPLE MOVING AVERAGES

Simple averages are constructed by totaling a series of data and dividing the total by the number of observations. For example, if I want to calculate a 10-day moving average, I would add up the closing prices for the last 10 days and divide the total by 10. This would give me the plot for today. To calculate the average for tomorrow, I would simply delete the close 10 days ago from the total, and add in tomorrow's closing price when it became available. The calculation is then repeated for each subsequent period, and that's how I get the average to "move."

If you look at Chart 7-1, of a 25-day moving average, you can see that it reverses direction well after the actual highs and lows in the price itself. This is because the average is plotted on day 25, but the average of the 25 periods actually takes place on day 13 (i.e., at the halfway point). Now if the average is to represent the underlying trend correctly, the latest calculation should really be centered (i.e., plotted on day 13). In Chart 7-2, I have plotted the solid line as a centered moving average. The dotted line is our original average. The arrows show that the centered moving average reverses direction first. In fact, the centered average offers some pretty good signals and reflects the underlying trend quite well. The problem can be seen from the right-hand part of the chart. There is no moving average for the last few periods because the data was not available. It is evident from this approach that a waiting time of 12 periods (in this case, days) is necessary before it is possible to know that the average has reversed direction. Time

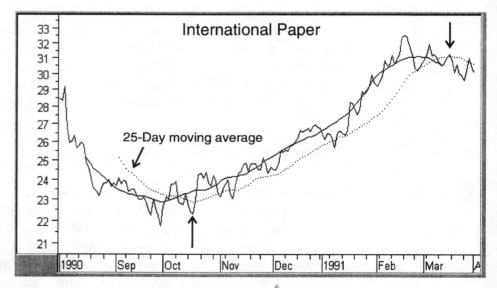

CHART 7-1. *International Paper.*

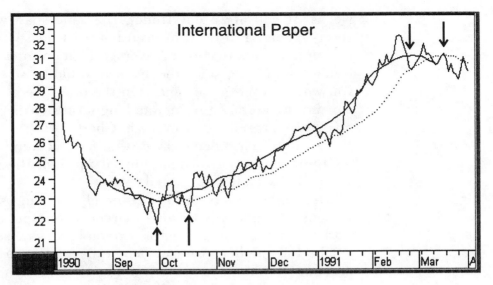

CHART 7-2.   *International Paper.*

delays cost money in markets, so technicians have discovered that better results are obtained when price reversal signals are generated when the price crosses above and below the non-centered moving average.

A bullish signal is given when the price crosses above the average, and a bearish one occurs when it moves below. This approach is far from perfect, but it is certainly more timely than waiting for a reversal in direction.

The choice of time span is critical when employing moving-average techniques. The first step is to decide which kind of trend you are trying to identify—normally short, intermediate, or long. Take another look at Figure 2-1 in Chapter Two for some perspective. The thick line represents the long-term or primary trend. You can see that the lows are separated by about a 4-year interval. This means that the primary trend lasts about a year, sometimes as short as 6 months, occasionally 2 years or longer. Long-term trends are interrupted by intermediate corrections, and these last from 6 weeks to 6 months. Finally, we have short-term trends that interrupt the intermediate ones. These span 2 to 3 weeks or as much as 6 weeks. If you are a day trader, the time span will be very short—a matter of days, or even hours. It doesn't make sense to use a 12-month moving average to monitor a short-term trend (Chart 7-3), since the average would be so smooth that you would never get a signal. On the other hand, using a 20-day moving average to generate long-term signals gives far too many whipsaws, as you can see in Chart 7-4.

Once you have determined what kind of trend to monitor, it's then a question of matching it up with the ideal span. Table 7-1 lists a few suggested spans.

Remember, there is, unfortunately, no time span for all seasons. What works for one market in one period may not work at another time. What is profitable for one security may not be for another. A lot of people have spent a substantial amount of time and money trying to establish ideal time spans, and all have failed. If you can recognize and deal with this fact right now, you will be much further ahead of the game. Don't go for the perfection that cannot be achieved. Instead, look for a span that works reasonably well over most markets most of the time. A moving average, after all, is

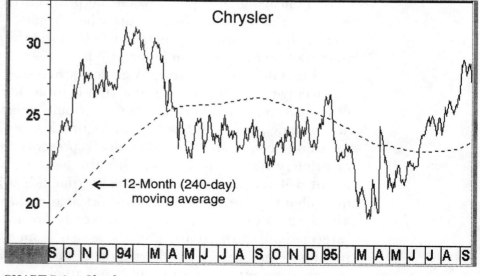

CHART 7-3. *Chrysler.*

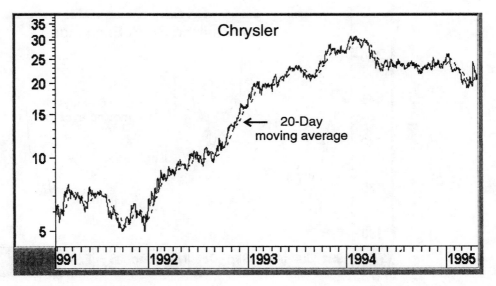

CHART 7-4.   *Chrysler.*

Table 7-1 Suggested Time Spans for Moving Averages (in Months)

Short-Term	Intermediate-Term	Long-Term
10	13	6
14	26	9
25	40	12
30	52	18
45	65	26

another technical tool, not the holy grail. Use it along with others like trendlines and price patterns.

One of the things to bear in mind when choosing a time span for a particular trend is that there is always a trade-off between *sensitivity and timeliness.* In Chart 7-5, the dotted line is a 65-day moving average. It gives reasonably reliable signals, because it has a relatively long time span. However, these crossovers often occur well after the peaks and troughs, as indicated by the arrows.

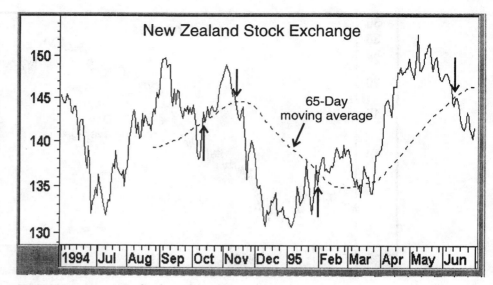

CHART 7-5. *New Zealand Stock Exchange.*

In Chart 7-6, the average has a 10-day span and gives very timely signals, but too many of them turn out to be costly whipsaws. Some of the worst are highlighted in the two boxes. The box on the right contains an especially nasty concentration of whipsaws. Chart 7-7 shows them in greater detail.

Chart 7-8 features both a 10-day and a 25-day moving average. The 10-day is the dotted line and the 25-day is the solid line. The 25-day span represents a compromise between the 10- and 65-day series. As you can see, quite a lot of whipsaws are generated by the 10-day crossovers. On the other hand, there are far fewer from the 25-day average. This happens to be a very good example. In most markets a 25-day crossover does not work as efficiently, so please bear this in mind.

RULES OF INTERPRETATION

Now it is time to look at some useful rules of interpretation for simple moving averages.

CHART 7-6.   *New Zealand Stock Exchange.*

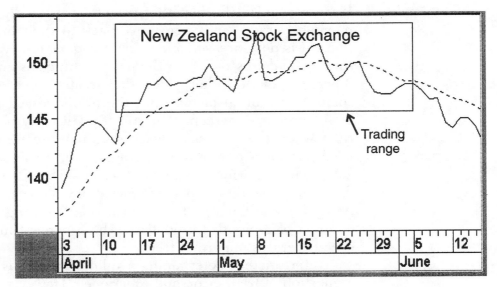

CHART 7-7.   *New Zealand Stock Exchange.*

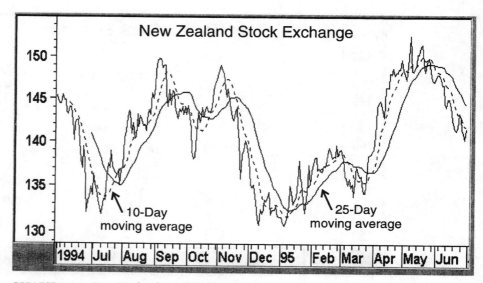

CHART 7-8.   *New Zealand Stock Exchange.*

RULE 1

If we recognize the fact that prices occasionally slip across moving averages and then move back to their original positions, it is not unreasonable to ask the question "What constitutes a valid crossover?" In the past, technicians employed the 3 percent rule. In other words, they treated the crossover with some degree of suspicion until the price crossed the average by a factor of 3 percent (Chart 7-9). This may have been all right when the time horizons were much greater and people used very long-term moving averages, as in this chart showing a 12-month moving average with cash soybeans. However, in day-to-day trading a 3 percent move may represent the entire trend. Look at Chart 7-10, for instance, featuring a perpetual contract of 3-month Eurodollars. The 3 percent move doesn't even cover this important trend.

Unfortunately, determining a valid crossover is very much a question of trial, error, and experience. However, there are a few guidelines which can be used. For example, look for a moving-average crossover to take place around the same time as a price pattern completion or a trendline violation.

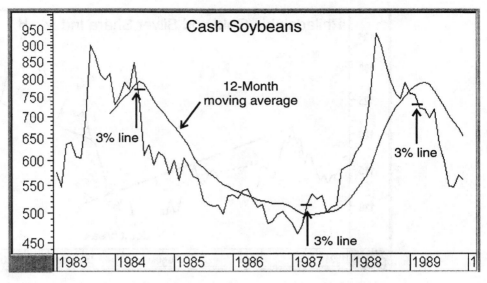

CHART 7-9.   *Cash soybeans.*

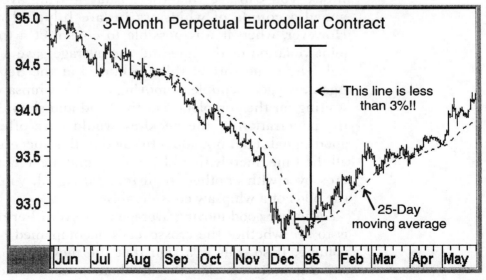

CHART 7-10.   *3-month perpetual Eurodollar contract.*

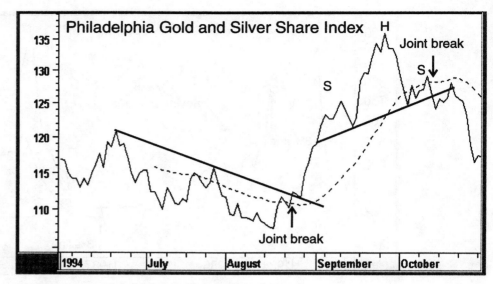

CHART 7-11.   *Philadelphia Gold and Silver Share Index.*

In Chart 7-11, of the Philadelphia Gold and Silver Share Index, you can see that the 25-day moving average experienced a couple of whipsaws in late July and mid-August. However, when it was possible to construct a trendline, the joint violation of the line and the average gave a reliable signal. The same sort of thing occurred at the September top. Again, we get a couple of moving-average whipsaws. However, waiting for the completion of the head-and-shoulders top with the penetration of the neckline would have offered a pretty good signal. I am not going to say that this success rate occurs all the time, merely that, if you can combine a moving-average crossover with another trend reversal signal, you will reduce the odds of a whipsaw considerably.

Another good moving-average crossover filtering technique is to see whether the crossover is accompanied by expanding volume. If so, this is a sign that the move is probably valid, since it indicates that the breakout is associated with some degree of optimism in the case of an upside breakout, or pessimism in the case of a downside crossover. Chart 7-12 shows the Israel First Fund, a closed-end investment fund on the

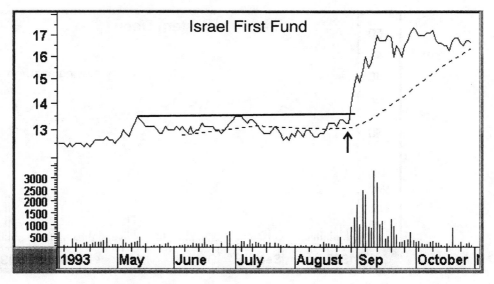

CHART 7-12. *Israel First Fund.*

NYSE. It broke above its 45-day moving average in mid-August, but it was not until a week later that the breakout became more decisive as the price rallied above the trendline, and more important, volume expanded considerably.

In Chart 7-13, showing Western Deep, a South African gold stock, we see that several whipsaws of the 45-day average occurred in November. Then in early December the price broke above the average again, but why should this breakout be any more believed than the others? The answer is it shouldn't, that is until the price pulled back, found support at the average and then rose again, but this time with considerable volum, as flagged by the arrows. It was the huge increase in volume that would have provided the confidence that the most recent breakout was valid.

Another filtering possibility is to wait for two periods to see whether the crossover holds. Quite often we find that the price moves across the average in what looks to be a valid move, only to find that in the next period (say, day), it moves back across the average. When it can maintain its crossover

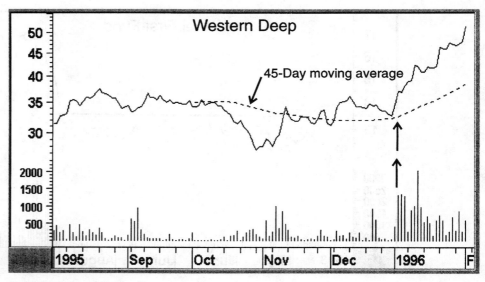

CHART 7-13.   *Western Deep.*

for more than one period, the odds are greater that the crossover will hold. In Chart 7-14, of the U.S. Dollar Index, the crossover at arrow 1 did not hold for even a day; neither did arrow 3. However, arrow 2 did hold for 2 days and then slipped back. Finally, arrow 4 experienced a successful retracement test. Then the price took off.

Let's look at arrow 2 again. I think that most people would agree that this was a decisive crossover, so why would we not have gone with it? In a strict sense, there is probably no reason, except to say that at this point the crossover had been in force for only one day. One reason the breakout could have been questioned is that the price never broke above its previous high, as indicated by the horizontal trendline. It's a small point, but represents the kind of thing you need to be on the lookout for. Remember, a moving-average crossover is one element of evidence that the trend has reversed. The failure of the price to rally above the previous high is a piece of evidence that offsets the crossover. In Chart 7-15 we take a closer look. You can see that the valid crossover at arrow 4 was accompa-

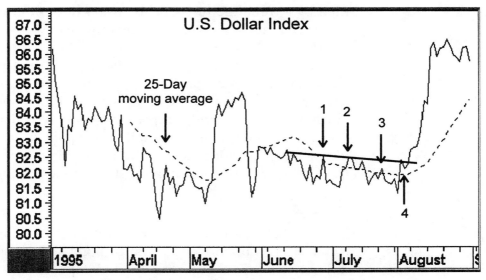

CHART 7-14.   *U.S. dollar.*

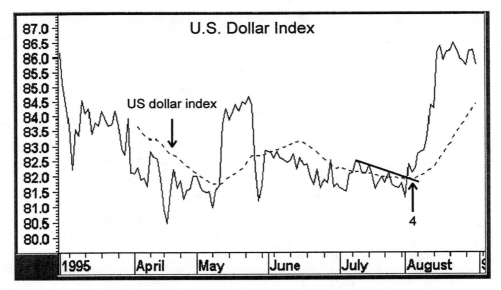

CHART 7-15.   *U.S. dollar.*

nied by a trendline break. This would have offered even more evidence that the moving-average crossover was valid.

You may have noticed that most of the charts I've used are based on closing prices. This is because closing prices reflect positions that traders are willing to take home overnight or over the weekend. Since it indicates a commitment on their part, closing prices generally represent a better reflection of the underlying trend than extreme intraday points. For this reason, it's usually a good idea to wait for the closing price to penetrate the average before concluding that the trend has reversed.

RULE 2

Since a moving average is designed to reflect an underlying trend, it is a support or resistance point in its own right. The difference between an actual level of support or resistance and a moving average is that the moving average represents a dynamic support or resistance zone, not a static one. Consequently, when the price falls to a moving average in a rising trend it is usually a good idea to assume that it will find support at the moving average. After all, one of the basic principles of technical analysis is that a trend is assumed to be in force until the weight of the evidence shows or proves that it has been reversed. In Chart 7-16, you see that the Canadian dollar touches or approaches its 65-week simple moving average on numerous occasions. Only where I have placed the arrows do we get a meaningful whipsaw during the 5-year bull market, but by and large the average works pretty well.

As with trendlines, the more times a moving average has been touched or approached without being violated, the greater its significance as a support or resistance area. Talking of trendlines, look at the late-1986 crossover. See how the two previous ones were whipsaws, but this one was valid. One reason—the price broke above the neckline of a reverse head-and-shoulders pattern.

RULE 3

In general, the longer the time span of the moving average, the greater the significance of the crossover. For example, a

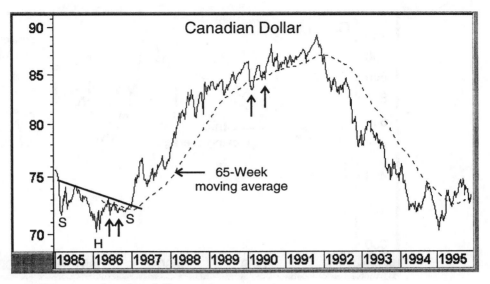

CHART 7-16. *Canadian dollar.*

crossover of a 15-day moving average has implications for the short-term trend, but not much more. On the other hand, a violation of a 40-week moving average may indicate a primary-trend reversal and therefore carries much more weight.

RULE 4

A crossover of a moving average with a sharp angle of ascent or descent has less significance than if the average is rising or falling slowly. The sharper the angle of ascent or descent, the more likely the crossover will turn out to be a whipsaw. In the weekly chart of the Italian Comit Index (Chart 7-17), arrow 1 shows a false breakdown from a moderately rising average. Arrow 2 is more striking in that the average was falling quite sharply and the breakout again was a whipsaw. The same sort of thing happened right at the end of 1982, where the breakout was unable to hold because of the sharp decline. Arrow 4 indicates how a sharply declining average often serves as important resistance for a rally. It is an excellent place to consider going short, because you can always use the average as a stop-loss point.

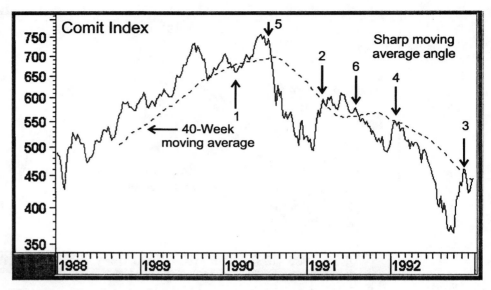

CHART 7-17. *Comit Index.*

Finally, arrows 4 and 5 are marked, not because they were bullish, but because they were reliable signals. Note how the 40-week moving average was fairly flat at the time. I do not wish to leave you with the idea that crossovers of flat averages are always reliable, and those of sharp up or down averages always result in whipsaws, for that is not true. The point is that penetrations of flat averages are more likely to be valid than those averages with a moderately sharp angle of ascent or descent. Indeed, in a trading range market, when moving-average crossovers are almost always false, the average is almost certain to be pretty flat. If the trading range can be easily identified, use the upper and lower boundaries, as these will be more reliable. In Chart 7-18, of the Japanese yen, the trading range is bounded by two horizontal lines. There are countless whipsaws triggered by the 25-day moving average, so once you realize that this is in fact a trading range, the two parallel trendlines are the places on which to focus, since their violations will offer the more reliable signals.

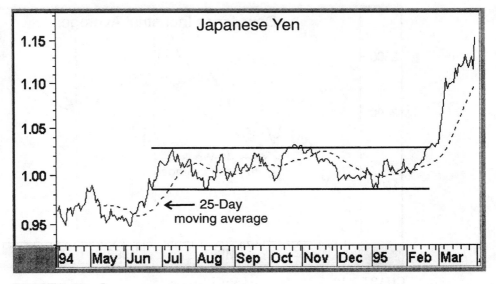

CHART 7-18. *Japanese yen.*

RULE 5

Reversals in the direction of a moving average are generally more significant than crossovers. The problem is that reversals usually come well after the fact. When they do, the reversals merely serve as a confirmation that you are on the right track. However, when you are lucky enough to spot a reversal fairly close to the final peak or trough, this is generally a very low-risk, high-reward signal. Chart 7-19, of the Dow Jones Industrial Average and a 40-week moving average, shows two extremes. The first is the change in direction following the 1987 crash, as flagged by the dashed vertical line. This reversal in direction was clearly much too much after the fact. On the other hand, the solid vertical line shows when it became obvious that the moving average had reversed direction to the upside. This was definitely a much more timely and reliable signal.

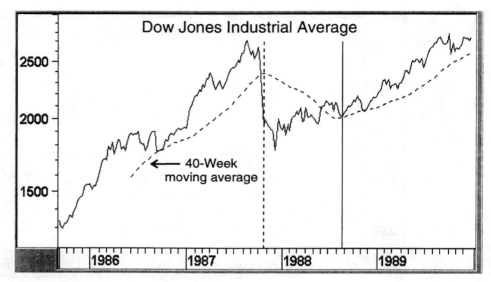

CHART 7-19.   *Dow Jones Industrial Average.*

FRONT-LOADED AVERAGES

Our second category of moving average is the front-loaded variety. These averages are constructed in several different ways, but one way or another each gives a greater weighting to more recent data. In this section we are going to take a quick look at one of them: the exponential moving average.

Exponential moving averages (EMAs) are calculated by multiplying the difference between today's price and a moving average, by an exponent. The value of the exponent varies with the chosen time span. Since all major charting packages automatically calculate an EMA for you, I'll skip over the method of calculation. The main thing to bear in mind is that an EMA is more sensitive and reverses direction ahead of a simple moving average of the same time span. Chart 7-20 shows two 30-day averages. The solid line is the simple average and the dashed line is the EMA. Arrows 1 and 2 show two points where the leading characteristics of the EMA are most evident.

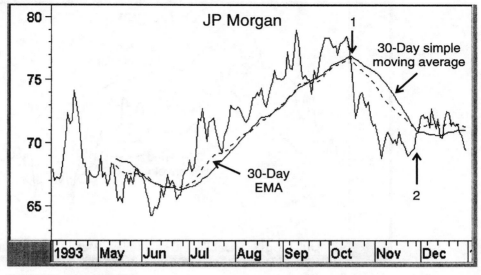

CHART 7-20.   *J. P. Morgan.*

Since the EMA is more sensitive, it offers more timely signals. However, since both moving-average time spans and methods of calculation are a trade-off between timeliness and sensitivity, this sensitivity does not come without a price—and that, of course, means a lot more whipsaws. It is my belief that it is best to keep things as simple as possible. In fact, I have seen no evidence in testing huge amounts of data that the EMA is any better than a simple moving average. For this reason, I find that the simple average is as good as any.

ENVELOPES AND BOLLINGER BANDS

One popular method of moving-average interpretation is to plot envelopes or bands around the moving average at a set interval, as in Chart 7-21. If the bands are selected carefully, they serve as support or resistance points. In effect, this approach plots a dynamic form of momentum indicator. As noted in the momentum discussion in Chapter Eight, the

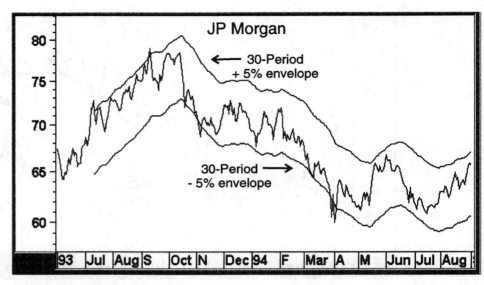

CHART 7-21.   *J. P. Morgan.*

envelopes act as a form of dog's leash. My own feeling is that these envelopes may look good on paper, but they have relatively little practical use since the price often exceeds the envelope boundaries.

Chart 7-21, however, does demonstrate one very helpful pointer. First of all, we have two simple moving averages at ± 5 percent of a 30-day moving average. Let's say the moving average itself was at 50. Then the + 5 percent average would be plotted at 52½ (i.e., 5 percent above the average). If you look at the period on the left, a bull market, you will see that the upper envelope was touched quite a bit, but the lower one not at all. When the lower one was touched for the first time, in October, it was a warning that the trend had changed to the downside. In fact, the price was never able to touch the upper, overbought envelope during the whole period of the decline, yet it did touch the lower envelope several times. The rule, then, is that periods are likely to be bearish when the upper envelope is not touched, and those when the lower line is not reached tend to be bullish.

Bollinger bands are an alternative to the envelope approach. They were developed by the innovative technician John Bollinger. Unlike envelopes, which are plotted as fixed percentages above and below a moving average, Bollinger bands are plotted as standard deviations (Chart 7-22). What this means in a practical sense is that the two bands expand and contract as the volatility of the price series changes.

The lower panel of this chart compares the price with two 20-day moving-average envelopes. The top panel does the same thing with 20-day Bollinger bands. The 20-day time span is recommended for shorter-term intermediate price moves. It is apparent that the Bollinger series in the upper panel is much more sensitive to price changes in sharp up or down trends.

Chart 7-23 eliminates the lower panel so that we can take a closer look at the Bollinger band. You can see that the price occasionally moves outside the band for a day or two, but is normally unable to sustain itself in this position. When the trend moves persistently in one direction, such as in early 1991 at arrow 1, touching the upper band no longer offers a

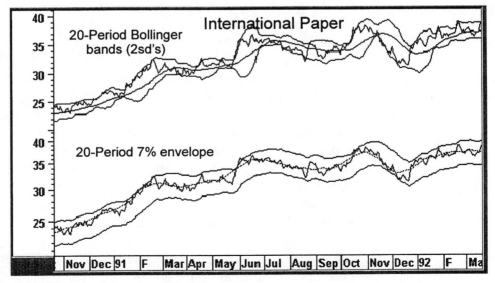

CHART 7-22. *International Paper.*

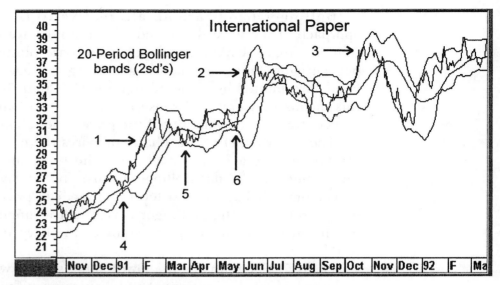

CHART 7-23. *International Paper.*

timely signal, in much the same way as a momentum indicator is virtually useless when a persistent trend is in force. This is the exception rather than the rule, for in most cases when the price moves above the band and then back below it, an exhaustion move has set in from which a correction follows. Look what happened to the price at arrow 2, and again at arrow 3. These were clearly great places to take profits.

Also, if you have a good idea from the other technical indicators of the direction of the primary trend, it's possible to use those few occasions when the price moves to the lower band to enter long in a short-term trade. Look at the arrows numbered 4, 5, and 6, and see what good opportunities they were.

There are several other interpretive points we could consider, on both Bollinger bands and moving averages in general, but unfortunately space does not permit. Those of you wishing for more information, should refer to the advanced CD-ROM course on technical analysis.

SUMMARY

1. The objective of a moving average is to smooth the data so the underlying trend becomes more obvious.

2. There are two types of moving averages: equally weighted and front-weighted.

3. Ideally, a moving average is centered, but because of the time lag involved in waiting for the final data, technicians generally use moving-average crossovers as buy and sell signals.

4. A good moving average acts as a dynamic support or resistance area.

5. A moving-average crossover gains its significance from the time span, the angle of ascent or descent, and the number of times it has been a successful support or resistance zone.

6. Moving-average reversals represent reliable, timely signals when they occur close to a trend's turning point.

PART THREE

ADVANCED TECHNIQUES

This section covers supplementary techniques that help support the trend reversal methods discussed in Part 2. The principles outlined in this part of the book should be used in conjunction with those in Part 2. The penultimate chapter describes Japanese candlesticks, a technical tool that has become popular, especially with futures and other short-term traders in the last few years. Finally, Chapter 12 brings a lot of the techniques together in an attempt to provide some practical trading tips.

PRINCIPLES
OF MOMENTUM

Over the years, technicians have developed many different indicators which attempt to measure the velocity of price moves, both up and down. These oscillators can be banded together under one heading: *momentum*. Momentum is one of the most frequently used techniques in technical analysis, but probably the least understood. In this chapter we will cover the basic principles of momentum interpretation, and in the next chapter describe some of the more popular individual indicators and how the principles apply to them.

Momentum measures the velocity of a price move. It is a generic term. Just as the word *fruit* encompasses apples, oranges, grapes, bananas, and so forth, *momentum* embraces a host of individual indicators such as rate of change (ROC), relative-strength indicator (RSI), moving-average convergence divergence (MACD), and stochastics (Figure 8-1). Each indicator has different attributes, but the principles of interpretation apply to all of them.

Let's take a closer look at the fruit analogy. Two common characteristics of fruit are that it is sweet and is almost always grown during the warmest season. Some kinds of fruit are sweeter than others, some require very hot temperatures, others need a long growing season, and so on. Momentum indicators also have common characteristics, but the indicators themselves, like the different kinds of fruit, differ individually in the way we interpret them. There are a large number of these interpretive rules. We will consider the five most important here. The advanced CD-ROM course on technical analysis will deal with all of them. At any rate, some indicators lend themselves to virtually all the rules; others, to only two or

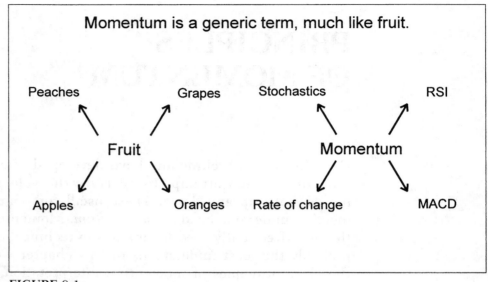

FIGURE 8-1.

three. We shall learn later, for instance, that the rate-of-change indicator lends itself to trendline construction, the RSI to overbought or oversold conditions, and so on.

The five momentum principles to be covered in this chapter are:

Overbought/oversold conditions

Divergences

Trendline violations

Price pattern completions

Moving-average signals

While we are going to spend quite some time studying momentum, it is important to remember that you cannot buy and sell momentum. You can buy and sell only the price. It follows, then, that buy and sell signals can come only from a reversal in trend of the actual price, not from a reversal in the momentum series. Momentum's valuable contribution is to tell us when the underlying technical structure is weakening or strengthening, thereby giving us advance warning when a reversal in price may be about to take place.

Please note that all the examples used in this chapter are of a nondescript or generic momentum indicator. The next chapter will discuss individual indicators using actual marketplace examples.

OVERBOUGHT AND OVERSOLD

All momentum series have the characteristics of an oscillator as they move from one extreme to another. This is illustrated in Figure 8-2. These extremes are known as overbought and oversold levels. In my seminars I often equate these zones with a leash attached to an unruly dog taking a walk. The animal continually strains at the leash, moving from one side of the walk to the other. One moment the dog roams to the curb on his extreme left and the next he scampers back toward the lawns on his right, as far as the leash will allow him. Market

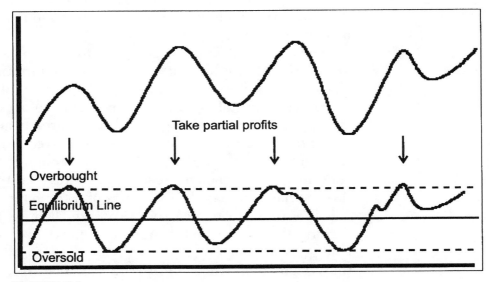

FIGURE 8-2.

momentum works in a similar manner, so that when an oscillator is at an overextended reading on the upside, it is said to
be *overbought*. When it reaches the opposite end of the spec-
trum on the downside, the condition is known as *oversold*.
The horizontal line in between these extremes is called the
equilibrium line, since it is the point of balance of the two
extremes.

Some indicators, such as the RSI, are calculated in such a
way that they have finite extremes above or below which the
oscillations cannot go. In these cases there is an established
default level for the overbought and oversold lines. Conversely,
other indicators such as the rate of change have no such theoretical boundaries, at least on the upside. Instead we must
insert the overbought and oversold lines on a trial-and-error
basis, using our best judgment. I'll give you some pointers for
this later, but for now, let me simply say that these lines
should be drawn so that the space between them includes the
bulk of the trading activity. In this case, try to think of the
oscillator as a rubber leash that from time to time will be
stretched beyond its normal length. Drawing lines to represent
the extremes is not particularly helpful. What we must do is
find the metaphorical equivalent of the end of the leash (i.e.,
the points that include most of the rallies and reactions in the
market under study).

The technical interpretation of overbought and oversold
lines is that they represent an intelligent point for anticipating
a trend reversal. An overbought condition is one in which you
should consider taking profits or reducing your exposure. For
example, if you are holding three gold contracts and the price
rallies to where it generates an overbought reading, you might
wish to take some partial profits. Even though the trend may
continue, the overbought reading indicates that the *odds* of a
reversal have increased. If the *risks* of a top have grown, then
it makes sense to reduce your exposure. If press stories concerning the bullish nature of the security are beginning to
emerge, and your emotions are telling you to buy more, use
these signs as further confirming evidence that it is a good
time to begin to *reduce* rather than *increase* your exposure.

On the other hand, if you believe that the main trend is down and you have been waiting for a short-term bounce as a time to sell, an overbought reading is as good a time as any. For the same reason, it would normally be a grave mistake even to consider making a purchase when an oscillator signals an overbought condition. The problem we all have is that this is precisely the time when most of us have the urge to buy, because rising prices attract optimism, positive news stories, and bullish sentiment.

The opposite is true for an oversold condition. Few people want to buy after prices have been falling and the news is inevitably discouraging. Unfortunately, that is the time when we need to control our shaking hands, pick up that phone, and call our friendly broker as shown by the upward pointing arrows in Figure 8-3*a*. That is also the moment when we should overcome, at all costs, the temptation to take a short position. In actual fact, the correct action is to cover part of any outstanding short positions (Figure 8-3*b*). At the time you may think that it is possible to make more money by holding on to your position, but believe me, taking some partial profits

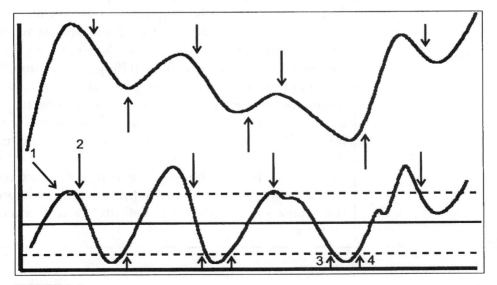

FIGURE 8-3*a*.

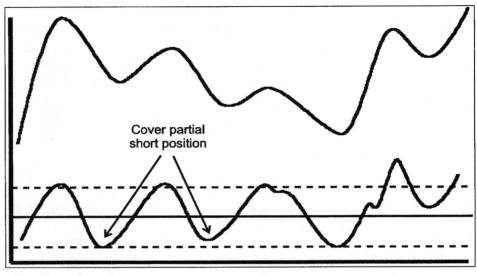

Cover partial
short position

FIGURE 8-3*b*.

A USEFUL TIP
Quite often a market trend will continue so that the oscillator goes well beyond the overbought or oversold extremes. In that event, it is often a good idea to wait for the indicator to recross the overbought or oversold line on its way toward zero and then take some action. You can see the possibilities in Figure 8-3*a*. See how selling at the time the indicator reaches the overbought zone at arrow 1 would have been premature. Waiting for the oscillator to recross the overbought zone at arrow 2 would have been far more profitable. The same was true for the oversold crossing at arrow 3. See how the momentum indicator recrossed its oversold line pretty close to the low at arrow 4. I'm not going to say that it works this well every time, because it doesn't, but the momentum approach is definitely a useful technique to employ.

will put you in a far more objective frame of mind when that inevitable rally gets under way.

THE IMPORTANCE OF TIME FRAMES

The importance of an overbought or oversold reading will depend on the time frame under consideration. For example, if the period used in constructing the indicator is 5 days, the implications from extreme readings will be nowhere near as profound as those from a momentum indicator spanning 12 months. Chart 8-1 shows an oscillator with a short time span on the left and a substantially larger one on the right. See how the overbought reading in the first indicator was followed by a decline of a few days, but the overbought reading in the one on the right was followed by a more substantial decline that took a lot longer to play out.

Momentum characteristics change with the direction of the primary trend. Oscillators that move in the direction of the primary trend not only tend to reach more extreme readings but maintain overbought conditions longer than those that move against the trend. In Figure 8-4, we see that the

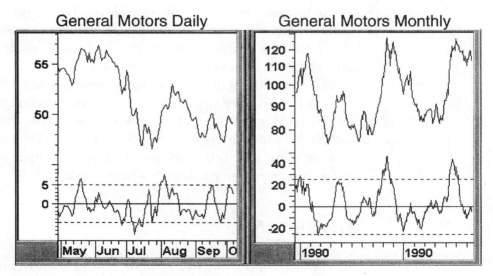

CHART 8-1. *General Motors daily/monthly.*

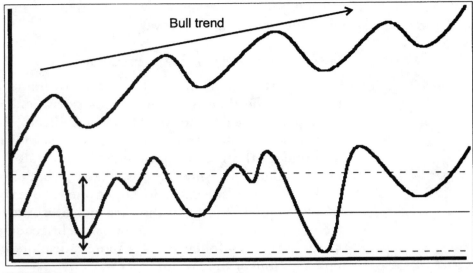

FIGURE 8-4.

main trend is up. Note how the overbought and oversold extremes are positioned equidistant from the equilibrium level indicated by the solid line. Rallies in the indicator have a tendency to move well into overbought territory and remain there for a longer time than do reactions. Reactions are almost always reversed at the oversold line or even sometimes before the oscillator reaches that point. This trait itself is a strong characteristic of a primary bull market.

The reverse will be true in a bear market (Figure 8-5). Rallies, when they are able to reach an overbought extreme, are usually terminated there. Reactions cause oversold readings to be much more extreme than normal. Whereas an oversold reading will normally generate a rally in a bull market, there is no such guarantee in a bear market.

DIVERGENCE

In the description of overbought and oversold conditions, we assume that the oscillator peaks and troughs were at roughly

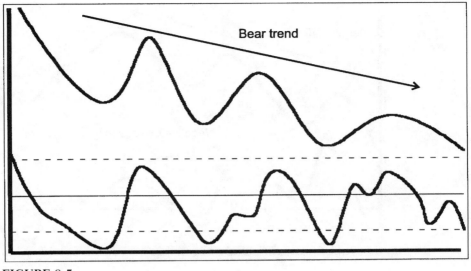

Bear trend

FIGURE 8-5.

the same time as the price. That is not often the case, however. An equally likely possibility is that the momentum indicator will turn ahead of the price. Think of a pen thrown into the air. The pen reaches its point of maximum velocity the instant it leaves the hand. It continues to rise—but at a slower and slower rate—until it is overcome by the force of gravity. Only then does it begin to fall back toward the ground.

All that a momentum indicator is trying to do, therefore, is to measure this acceleration and deceleration factor and present it in a graphic format. Figure 8-6 shows how this works in practice for a rising market. Point A marks the moment of maximum velocity, but the price itself continues to rally at a slower and slower pace until point C. This conflict between momentum and price is known as a *divergence*, since the oscillator is out of sync with the price. It is called a *negative* divergence, because rising prices are supported by weaker and weaker underlying momentum. The deteriorating momentum represents an early warning of some underlying weakness in the price trend.

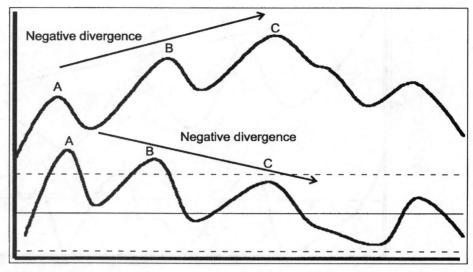

FIGURE 8-6.

In one respect markets are like houses: They take longer to build than to tear down. Markets spend most of their time advancing rather than declining. This means that *the lead characteristics of momentum indicators are usually more pronounced at market peaks than at troughs.*

Even so, divergences also occur at market bottoms, where they are called *positive,* because momentum hits bottom before the price. This phenomenon may be likened to a car in neutral gear being pushed over a hill. As the vehicle progresses down the slope, it gradually picks up speed or momentum. Then, as the gradient levels toward the bottom of the hill, the car slows down. Even though the speed is decreasing, the car itself continues to move before it finally slows to a halt. In this example, the speed of the car should be thought of as market momentum and its position as the price.

In Figure 8-7 the price is declining between points A and B, but at a slower and slower rate. The technical position is said to be improving or getting stronger. Indeed, if you think a market is in the process of reaching its bottom and you do not see a divergence, you may want to reconsider your analysis,

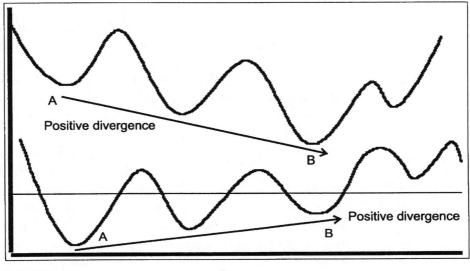

FIGURE 8-7.

because most market bottoms for any time span are preceded by at least one positive divergence.

HOW TO TELL THE SIGNIFICANCE OF A DIVERGENCE

There are three factors which help to establish the significance of a divergence. These are the number of divergences, the time span separating them, and the closeness of the momentum reading to the equilibrium level at the final turning point in price. Let's consider each one in turn.

Generally speaking, the more divergences which occur the greater their significance. In the case of a market peak, a large number of negative divergences indicates a trend that is undergoing a very long and serious weakening process.

The same principle applies to positive divergences at market bottoms. The more plentiful they are, the stronger the technical position.

The length of time separating the divergences is important because it reflects the type of trend you are monitoring. For example, if traders are analyzing short-term price movements, they would expect the divergences to take place over the course of a week or so at most. On the other hand, investors are principally concerned with the primary trend, so they would look for divergences associated with a momentum graph constructed from an intermediate trend time frame. In this case, three divergences in an intermediate oscillator are obviously more significant than three divergences in a short-term trend momentum series.

A final important point relates to the level at which the last divergence takes place. Generally speaking, the closer the last divergence to the equilibrium line, the more significant the divergence. At market peaks, rallies in a momentum indicator which are barely able to move above the zero level are often followed by a very sharp decline, as shown in Figure 8-8. This is one of the few instances in technical analysis when a clue appears hinting at the character of the next move. I must stress that such instances are not *always* followed by a sharp drop. Remember, technical analysis is far from perfect. However, in most cases when weak momentum of this nature is confirmed by a trend break in the price, be on your guard for a larger-than-normal selloff.

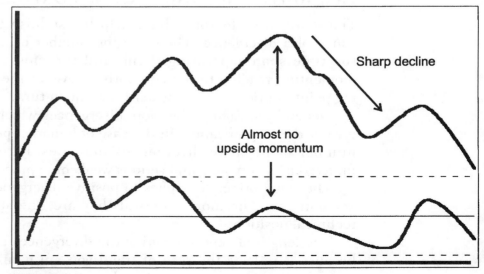

FIGURE 8-8.

The same principle, in reverse, holds for market bottoms. These occur when the price hits a new low following a number of positive divergences. In this case, though, the latest decline barely takes the momentum indicator below the equilibrium point. Once such action has been confirmed by a positive break in the price trend, an explosive advance usually follows.

Figure 8-9 shows the kind of situation I am driving at. See how the price makes a new low at point A. However, the momentum series barely falls below zero and a sharp rally follows.

DIVERGENCES MUST BE CONFIRMED BY PRICE

Perhaps the most important point to remember is that it is of paramount importance whether a divergence is confirmed by a trend break in the price itself. This, no matter how significant the divergence may appear, is based on our three rules.

Think of it this way: The darker the clouds, the heavier the rain shower. However, you don't know it's going to rain until you can hold your hand out and feel it, because there is

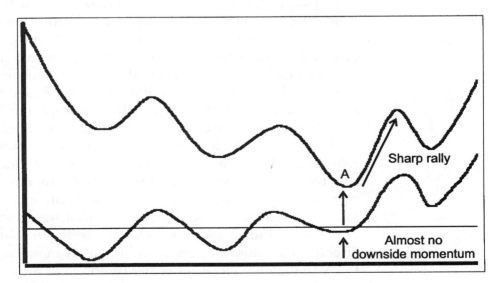

FIGURE 8-9.

always the chance that a new front will come in and blow the clouds away. The same is true for the relationship between price and momentum. One divergence can lead to another, and so forth.

Confirmation by a trend break in the price can come in many forms: trendline violations, moving-average penetrations, price pattern completions, and more. For example, the completion of any reversal price pattern signals a change in trend. However, the more divergences that precede this break—when combined with the other principles of momentum significance discussed above—the more emphasis is placed on the significance and intensity of the price pattern completion.

TRENDLINE VIOLATIONS

Momentum, like price, moves in trends. This means that the techniques used for analyzing price trends can be used for appraising momentum trends. Despite this fact, we must keep in mind that a trend reversal in momentum is usually, though not always, associated with a similar reversal in the price itself. Occasionally, an analysis of an oscillator trend will accurately tell us that momentum has reversed, and a reversal in price may indeed follow. However, the lag between the signal of a reversal in momentum and the actual turning point in price may be so great that trading decisions based on this signal will be unprofitable. That's why it is important to wait for a confirmation of a trend reversal in the price series itself.

In Figure 8-10, it is possible to construct a trendline that joins several bottoms in the momentum series (line 1). When the trendline is violated, the uptrend in momentum is reversed. Of course, this tells us only about momentum and nothing about the trend in price. For that we must try to isolate some kind of trend reversal as well. One of the most effective techniques I have found in all my momentum work is to try to match a violation of the trendline in momentum with a similar violation in price (line 2). When both are penetrated

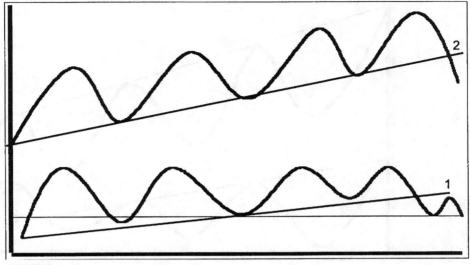

FIGURE 8-10.

the market usually reverses trend or, at the very least, consolidates for a while. In effect, the momentum signal represents additional confirmation in our weight-of-the-evidence
theory of trend reversals, discussed in earlier chapters.

Generally speaking, the more significant the momentum
trendline, the stronger the possibility that it will be followed
by an important reversal in price. The rules for ascertaining
the significance of a momentum trendline are identical with
those for assessing the importance of a trendline of the
price. As a reminder, they are (1) the length of the line, (2)
the number of times the line has been touched, and (3) the
angle of ascent or descent. If the trendline for price is just as
impressive, then the odds of a major reversal relative to the
time span under consideration will be that much greater.

In Figure 8-11, you can see the same principle in action.
This time the trend is reversing from down to up. See how
the momentum trendline is violated first. This provides us
with a warning. Later on a similar trendline for the price is
also violated, and a signal given.

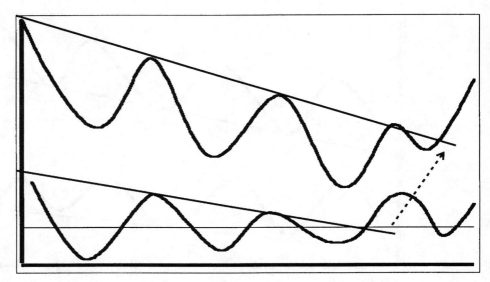

FIGURE 8-11.

PRICE PATTERN COMPLETION

Price formations do not occur very often in oscillators, but when they do it is time to sit up and pay attention, because these patterns usually result in worthwhile moves (Figure 8-12). I want to stress once again that the momentum reversal is just that—a reversal in momentum, not in price. However, when a momentum and price patterns reversal is confirmed by a trend break in the price, it almost always has important consequences—relative to the time frame under consideration, of course.

Price patterns in momentum indicators take the standard forms: rectangles, head and shoulders, triple tops, triangles, and so forth. The same principles used in price analysis also apply. For example, any formation gains its significance from its size and depth. However, since trends in momentum are, generally speaking, less sustainable than trends in price, momentum configurations are not as large and they are certainly far less plentiful. You can see a possibility in Figure 8-13,

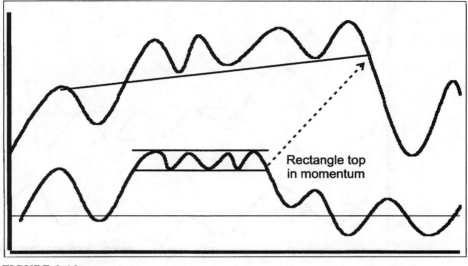

Rectangle top
in momentum

FIGURE 8-12.

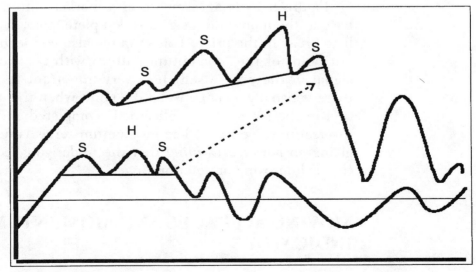

FIGURE 8-13.

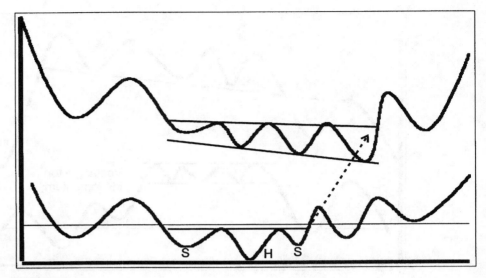

FIGURE 8-14.

where a head-and-shoulders top develops first in the momentum indicator and is later confirmed by one in the price series.

Figure 8-14 is an example of a market bottom where the base in the momentum series is completed, as later confirmed by a break in the price. This example also connects the breakout point of the momentum pattern with the trend reversal signal in the price itself. It is very important to understand there is usually a lag between the point when the price formation in the momentum indicator is completed and the actual reversal in price itself. The momentum series is nearly always giving an *advance warning* that the underlying technical picture is improving or deteriorating.

MOVING AVERAGES AND MOMENTUM INDICATORS

Because raw momentum indicators are often quite jagged and seemingly random affairs, the practice of smoothing them with moving averages has evolved. This makes it easier to get a better sense of the underlying momentum trend. The problem is that most raw momentum series are still too jagged to use the normal moving-average crossover technique, since a considerable number of whipsaws result. That is fairly obvious from Figure 8-15.

Consequently, many technicians plot two moving averages: a short one and one with a longer time span (Figure 8-16). Momentum buys and sells are then signaled (by the arrows) when the shorter-term moving average (the solid line) crosses above the longer-term one (the dashed line). Again, I stress that these are momentum buys and sells and should be continued by a trend break in the price.

SUMMARY

1. Momentum is a generic term which includes a number of different indicators. It measures the velocity of a price move, often giving advance warning of latent strength and weakness in a specific price trend.

2. The principles of momentum interpretation apply in some measure to all types of oscillators.

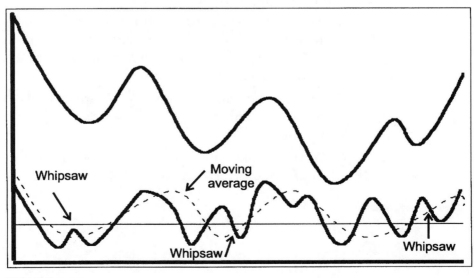

FIGURE 8-15.

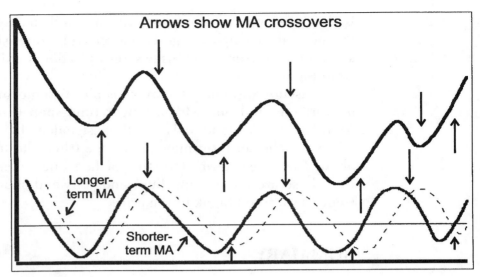

FIGURE 8-16.

3. Extreme readings and momentum divergences do not, in and of themselves, represent actual buy or sell signals. These can come only from a trend reversal in the price itself. Momentum characteristics do, however, emphasize the significance of such price signals when they are given.

4. Trend-determining techniques, normally used to spot reversals in price trends, can be applied to momentum indicators. These include trendlines, price patterns, and moving-average crossovers.

5. Trend reversals in momentum are usually followed by a trend reversal in the price, but normally with a lag between the two.

6. Always make sure that trend reversals in momentum are confirmed by price action.

KEY MOMENTUM INDICATORS

In this chapter we will apply the principles we learned in Chapter Eight by considering four widely followed oscillators. These are rate of change (ROC), relative-strength index (RSI), stochastics, and moving-average convergence divergence (MACD). Since all the popular charting packages allow you to plot these indicators, I'll be skipping over the actual formulas to save time and make things simpler. I'll begin then, with the rate of change.

RATE OF CHANGE

Rate of change is probably the easiest momentum indicator to construct. Do not let this fool you, however, as I consider it one of the most effective. Many people believe that a mathematically complex indicator will be superior to one derived from a simple formula. This is not the case. Some may be, but most are not. We all have a tendency to substitute the crutch of complexity for the effort of thinking. The golden rule of technical analysis is: *Do not cast away an indicator just because it is simple; reject it because it doesn't work.*

Rate of change calculation (ROC) compares the price today with the price *n* periods ago. For example, a 10-day ROC is calculated by comparing the price today with the price 10 days ago. Tomorrow's price would be compared with that of 9 days ago, and so forth. The result is then plotted as a continuous series which oscillates above and below the equilibrium level, as in Chart 9-1. The longer the time span used, the greater the fluctuation in the indicator, in terms of both magnitude and duration.

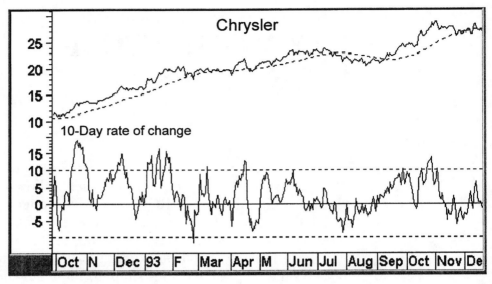

CHART 9-1. *Chrysler.*

OVERBOUGHT AND OVERSOLD LEVELS

The ROC indicator lends itself handsomely to overbought and oversold interpretations. The problem is there are no hard-and-fast rules about where the lines should be drawn, since the magnitude of the oscillations will vary according to the volatility of the underlying security and the time span being considered.

For this reason, overbought and oversold lines are constructed on a custom, or judgment, basis. Wherever possible, it is important to place them equidistant from the equilibrium level. This is because fear and greed tend to move in proportion and should be represented graphically in this way.

In general, we want the overbought and oversold extremes to correspond with the end of the dog leash described in the previous chapter. Unfortunately, the ROC oscillator represents a rubber leash, so it is necessary to be a little creative. Ideally, the lines should be drawn at such a level that they encompass as many large rallies and reactions as possible, yet do not include so many fluctuations as to dilute the sense of over-

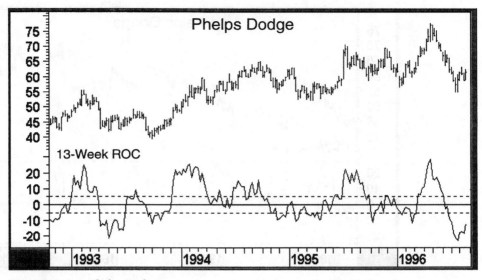

CHART 9-2. *Phelps Dodge.*

bought and oversold. In Chart 9-2 the lines are too close to the equilibrium level, since they include virtually every rally and reaction. Overbought and oversold readings therefore have no real practical use.

The lines in Chart 9-3, on the other hand, are too far apart. They certainly include the very sharp rally at the beginning, but nothing else is included. They also are of little practical use. In Chart 9-4 the lines are not perfect, but in a commonsense way they are a reasonable compromise, since they are close to most of the extreme points.

TRENDLINE CONSTRUCTION

Most rate-of-change (ROC) indicators are fairly jagged. This means it is sometimes difficult to spot trend reversals. On the other hand, their jaggedness makes the construction of trendlines that much easier. ROC is one of the most useful interpretive techniques of trendline analysis. You can see a couple of momentum trendlines in Chart 9-5. When the violations

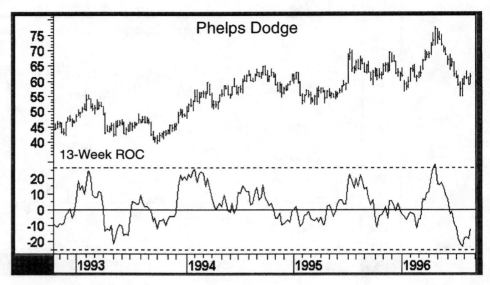

CHART 9-3. *Phelps Dodge.*

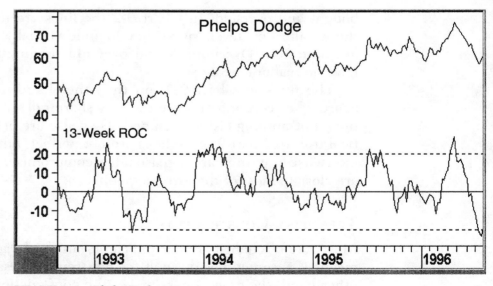

CHART 9-4. *Phelps Dodge.*

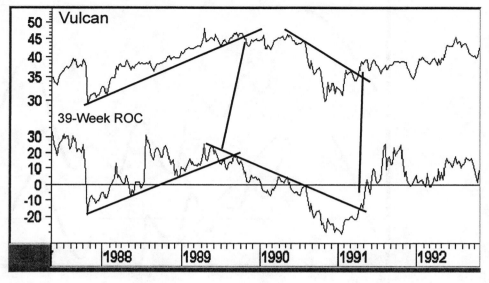

CHART 9-5. *Vulcan.*

are subsequently confirmed by a price trend reversal, you get some rather nice signals. While the trendline penetration in the ROC indicator does not actually represent a sell signal, it does give you timely advance warning of a likely trend reversal.

One note of caution here. It is possible for ROC indicators to move to unusual extremes, well beyond the normal overbought or oversold experience. This means it is often very easy to construct a very steep trendline joining two or three reversal points (Figure 9-1). Since the lines are very sharply angled, and the extreme connecting point is somewhat random, a degree of caution should be exercised in the interpretation of such violations.

Figure 9-2 shows a different trendline constructed from the same data. This one has a lower angle of descent and has been touched or approached on more occasions than the one in Figure 9-1. It is thus a far more suitable candidate.

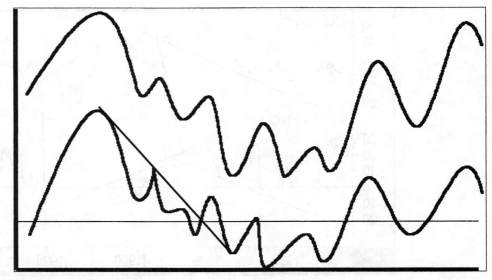

FIGURE 9-1.

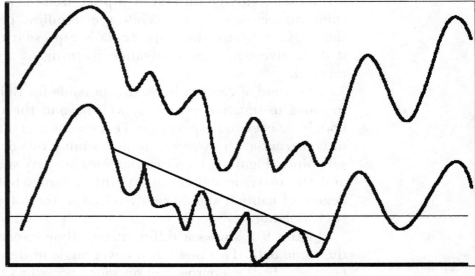

FIGURE 9-2.

PRICE PATTERNS

One of the key attributes of ROC indicators is they readily lend themselves to price pattern construction. In Chart 9-6, which extends back a number of years, there are two such patterns. When the breakouts are confirmed by a trend break in price, some pretty worthwhile moves develop. Also, note that although the chart covers a fairly long period, only two patterns are formed—demonstrating that such phenomena are somewhat rare. Even so, they are well worth looking for, since the resulting trend reversals are normally very significant.

Always remember to look at the level where the breakout occurs, for a pattern completion that develops near an overbought level in a rising trend is far less likely to work than one that takes place at an oversold or even neutral level. The opposite is true for a reversal in a declining market. You can see in Figure 9-3 that the trend on the left develops at a moderately oversold reading and is followed by a good move. On the other hand, since the odds do not favor strong price moves develop-

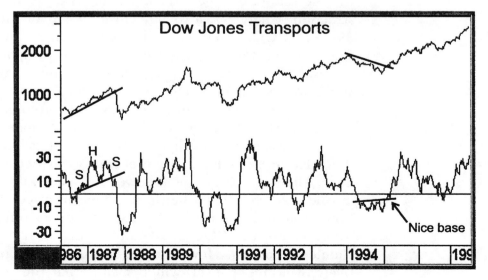

CHART 9-6. *Dow Jones Transports.*

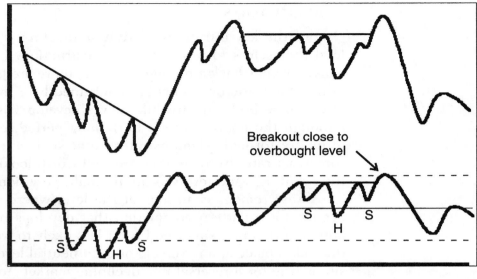

Breakout close to
overbought level

FIGURE 9-3.

ing after an overbought-reading price pattern, breakouts usually result in whipsaws, as is the case in this instance.

The rate-of-change indicator lends itself to trendline construction. Chart 9-7, a weekly closing chart of the yen and a
39-week ROC, shows several examples in the marketplace.
The 39-week time span is very useful for bringing out ROC
reversal characteristics. I also like 13- and 26-week spans.
You'll notice that these are all based on calendar quarters. Of
the three, the 9-month or 39-week variety often gives the best
results, perhaps because of the 9-month human birth cycle
and its emotional and physical characteristics. In 1985 both
the price and the ROC simultaneously violated down trendlines. This joint break was followed by a nice rally. As a general rule, it seems that when a trendline in price and momentum are simultaneously violated, the effect is stronger.

Later on, the ROC breaks out from a reverse head-and-
shoulders pattern. However, the breakout develops at a relatively overbought level, which means that the signal is suspect. In this case it certainly was, since the price rallied only

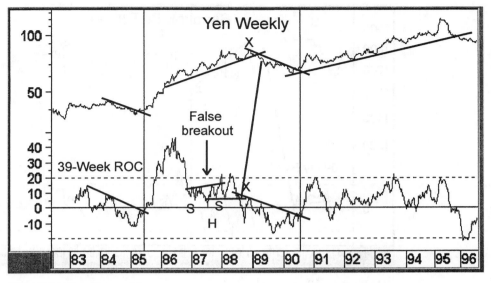

CHART 9-7. *Yen weekly.*

marginally and then peaked for the move. For this reason, it is always important to make sure that bullish price pattern breakouts occur either just above or just below the equilibrium level. In mid-1988 the ROC broke down from a top formation (i.e., below the horizontal line). This was the first warning sign from the indicator. It was later followed by the extremely weak momentum rally that occurred at the final peak at X. Typically, when a price reaches a new high after a good run, but momentum is barely able to struggle above its equilibrium level, a nasty decline follows once a price reversal signal has been given. In this case, the trendline violation in early 1989 served as the confirmation of both the top completion and the weak momentum rally. Normally we would expect to see a much sharper sell-off from such a nasty momentum combination. In this case, the price declined only about 12 percent from the break. Finally, we see a joint trendline penetration in mid-1990, only this time it's a bullish one.

Chart 9-8 features the Bangkok SET Index. This time we are using daily data with a 10-day ROC. If you look at the

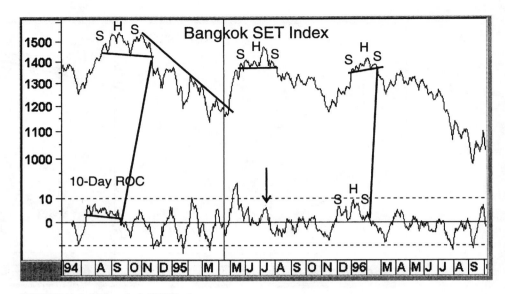

CHART 9-8. *Bangkok SET Index.*

three price peaks, you will see that each was associated with a
head-and-shoulders top. The first one was preceded by a top
formation in the 10-day ROC. The break occurred in mid-
September, but we had to wait about 2 months for the price to
confirm in November.

The next event was a positive divergence between the rate
of change and the price in April 1995. See how the ROC bottoms in January and the price reaches its low a couple of
months later. Then a very good downtrend line in the price is
violated. See how it was touched or approached on close to
eight occasions. Later, the high of the next rally was associated with a very weak momentum rally. It was also a negative
divergence, since the momentum peak was seen in May 1995.
The confirmation for this weak momentum came from the
break in the neckline of the head-and-shoulders top referred
to earlier.

Unfortunately, there was nothing in the chart to indicate
the November 1995 bottom—no timely, meaningful trendlines
or price patterns in either the price or the rate of change. The

next rally peak was well signaled, though, because the ROC traced out a head-and-shoulders top, the neckline of which developed around the zero level. This was simultaneously confirmed with a similar pattern breakdown by the price.

Ten-day time spans are helpful in the reading of daily charts, as are 14-, 25-, 30-, and even 45-day spans. A 45-day span appears in Chart 9-9, of the Dow Jones Index for the Finnish market. Since swings in these longer time spans are more deliberate, they often throw up important characteristics that are not apparent in the shorter 10- or 14-day spans. In this instance, we can see a joint simultaneous break by the ROC and the price in April 1994. Then a break by the ROC at the end of July from an extreme overbought condition warns of possible trouble ahead. The signal was then confirmed by the price as it violated the dashed uptrend line. The price itself did not immediately respond, because it rallied back to resistance in the form of the extended line.

However, the peak was associated with a very small momentum rally in the area of the extended trendline. This

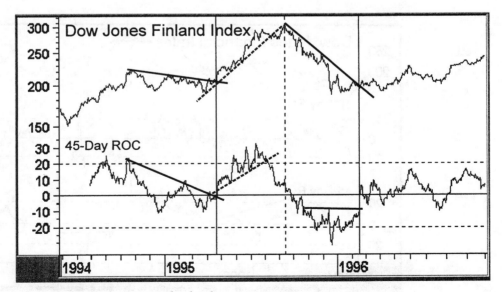

CHART 9-9. *Dow Jones Finland Index.*

was a very intelligent place to anticipate a peak, because the price was at resistance and a momentum uptrend had already been violated. Finally, the very weak rally warned of an impending sharp drop, once the price had reconfirmed, which it did with a break below the more or less horizontal trendline in early October 1995.

Finally, in February 1996, the ROC broke out from a reverse head-and-shoulders pattern at the same time that the price violated a very good downtrend line. Normally I would have expected a much more formidable rally from such a positive momentum/price combination, but that again goes to show that technical analysis is not perfect.

One useful tip is to combine two or more momentum indicators on one chart. In this way, not only is it possible to detect momentum reversal characteristics that may not be apparent by just looking at one indicator, but in the case where both series are giving reversal signals, the warning of a trend reversal is that much stronger. Chart 9-10 shows a 10-day and a 45-day ROC. See how both series violate trendlines in the March–April 1995 period, thereby signaling the rally

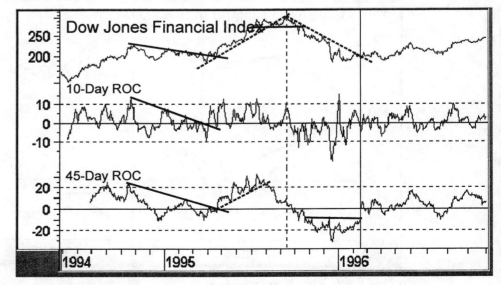

CHART 9-10.   *Dow Jones Financial Index.*

once the price also confirmed. Later on, in early August, the break in the 45-day series foretold of trouble, but notice that the 10-day indicator did not violate any important trendlines. In February 1996, the same absence of a price pattern or trendline break occurred for the 10-day series, unlike the 45-day ROC, which did complete a reverse head-and-shoulders pattern. However, the 10-day series did experience a dramatic swing from oversold to overbought, which its 45-day counterpart did not pick up. Often these dramatic swings are associated with very important market turning points.

THE RSI

The RSI, commonly known as the relative-strength indicator (Chart 9-11), is a momentum series and should in no way be confused with the *principle of relative strength,* in which one series is divided by another. It is a front-weighted price velocity ratio for a specific security relative to itself and is therefore relative to its past performance.

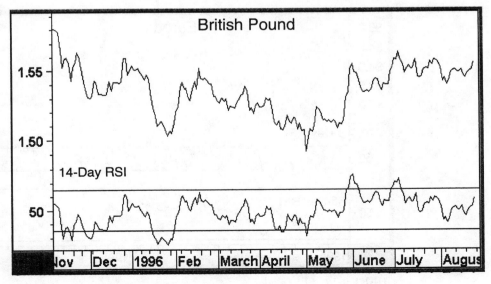

CHART 9-11. *British pound.*

If you recall our analogy of the dog and the leash in the last chapter, you will remember that one of the problems of momentum indicators is that it is possible for them to move to unusual extremes—in effect, reflecting a rubber leash. The RSI does not suffer from this drawback, since its calculation results in absolute levels being set at 100 and 0, although in practice they are rarely attained. With the RSI it is possible to gauge whether one security is more volatile than another by comparing their vertical movement, both up and down.

With a 14-period default, the oversold and overbought levels are traditionally set at 30 for oversold and 70 for overbought.

It is important to note that the volatility of the RSI moves inversely to that of most other momentum series. This means that for very short time periods the fluctuations are much greater. Look at Chart 9-12 for a 9-day RSI. See how the oversold and overbought readings are often attained and usually well exceeded. Now look at the 65-period RSI. The indicator never reaches the overbought and oversold zones. This means that these bands should be narrowed for longer-term time

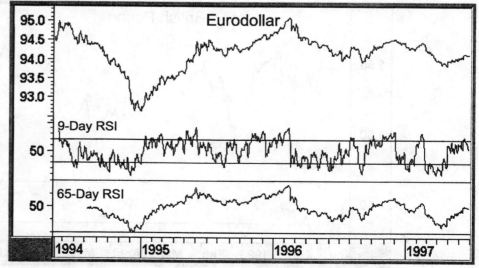

CHART 9-12. *Eurodollar.*

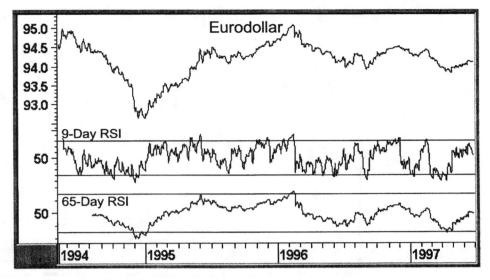

CHART 9-13. *Eurodollar.*

spans. Something on the order of 65/35 would be more appropriate. In Chart 9-13, I have changed the bands and you can see how the new lines better reflect the extreme fluctuations in the indicator.

INTERPRETING THE RSI

Many of the basic principles of momentum interpretation described in the previous chapter apply to the RSI. I'll discuss six of them.

1. *Tops and bottoms* (Figure 9-4). Wells Wilder, the inventor of the RSI, points out that tops are demonstrated when the indicator goes above 70 and bottoms when it falls below 30. This, of course, is another way of expressing the overbought and oversold characteristics described earlier. Since momentum typically turns ahead of price, these "tops" and "bottoms" often give advance warning of a strengthening or deterioration in the underlying technical structure. The 70/30 combination

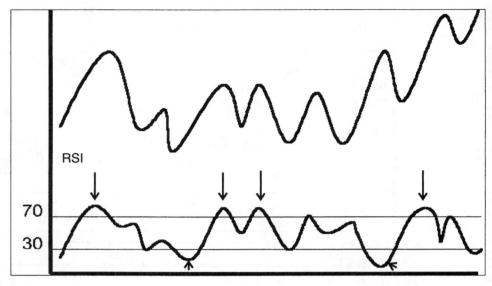

RSI

70

30

FIGURE 9-4.

assumes a 14-period time span, so longer-term time spans—say, above 25 days—would use a narrower overbought and oversold zone.

2. *Chart formations* (Figure 9-5).   The RSI is one of the few indicators that lend themselves to chart pattern construction. Formations do not appear to develop as plentifully as in the ROC indicator, but they nevertheless represent a useful addition to the RSI analysis. Chart 9-14 shows a classic example using a 14-day RSI for the pound. Note how the September 1992 peak was associated with a giant head-and-shoulders top in the RSI. Once the neckline at 50 was penetrated and the trendline in the currency itself was violated, there was only one way in which the currency could go.

3. *Failure swing—rising trend* (Figure 9-6).   The failure swing in a rising trend occurs when the RSI moves toward the equilibrium level, having already registered an overbought reading. It then moves back to overbought territory; but this

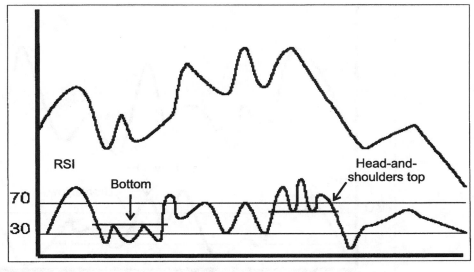

FIGURE 9-5.

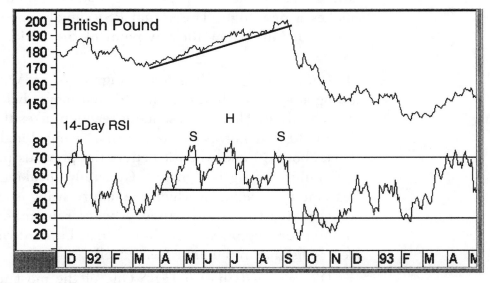

CHART 9-14.   *British pound.*

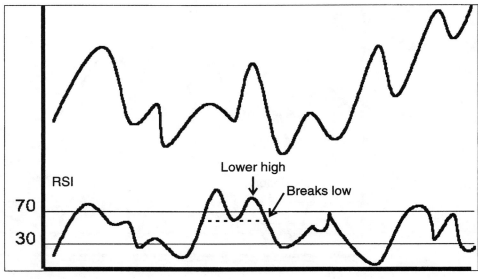

FIGURE 9-6.

swing fails to reach the peak of the first, even though the price makes a new high. The actual RSI signal comes when the indicator falls below the low point of the initial overbought swing.

4. *Failure swing—falling trend* (Figure 9-7).   With a failure swing at a market bottom, the RSI first moves below 30, then back above it. Then a subsequent reaction takes the RSI back below 30, but not as far as the first swing. Finally it rallies back above 30 and when it betters the previous peak, a positive failure swing is signaled. Generally speaking, the more extreme the reading at which the failure swing is experienced, the greater the significance. Always remember, this is a momentum signal which should also be confirmed with a reversal signal in the price trend itself.

5. *Divergences* (Chart 9-15).   One of the most useful functions of the RSI is to point up divergences between the price and momentum. Examples of divergences are widespread, but

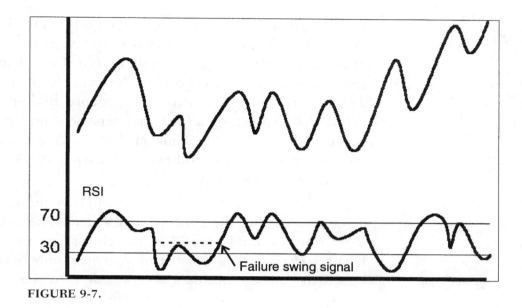

FIGURE 9-7.

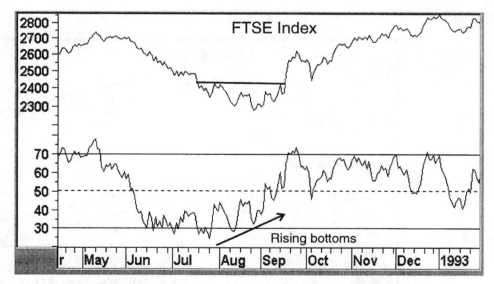

CHART 9-15.   *FTSE Index.*

in particular we might consider the August–September bottom in the FTSE Index. The actual low in late August was preceded by an RSI that had begun to walk up hill. Even more impressive was the fact that each time the index itself touched the 2375 area, the RSI continued to record higher numbers. While this characteristic does not represent an actual divergence, it does reflect the concept that the longer the trend of improving momentum following a sharp setback, the more bullish the technical position.

6. *Trendlines* (Chart 9-16).   Experience in the marketplace demonstrates that the concept of RSI trendline construction is an unquestionably valid approach, as you can see from Chart 9-16. However, because of the constraints of the formula, which limit the upside and downside extremes to 100 and 0 respectively, trendline construction is less applicable in a relative sense, to the RSI than the ROC. The RSI seems to come into its own more as an overbought/oversold and divergence indicator.

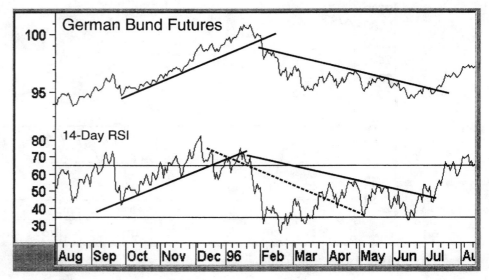

CHART 9-16.   *German Bund futures.*

EXAMPLES

Chart 9-17 shows a 14-day RSI of the closed-end Latin American Discovery Fund. There are a couple of points to cover. On the extreme left is a series of positive divergences. See how the RSI bottoms in October 1995 and gradually makes a series of rising bottoms. At the same time, the price is tracing out a series of declining lows. This set of positive divergences is eventually confirmed by the price trend break. Adding to the strength of the signal is the break in the declining trendline of the RSI in November 1995.

The other feature of the chart is the overbought crossover in February 1996. Quite often, when the RSI spends some time in a trading range above the overbought zone and then crosses back down on its way toward the equilibrium level (50 in Chart 9-17), the price will also decline. This is precisely what happened here. However, it is important to note that it was not really possible to construct a meaningful trendline for the price, only a very small secondary uptrend line, so a classic sell signal was never given. Sometimes you have to use a bit of

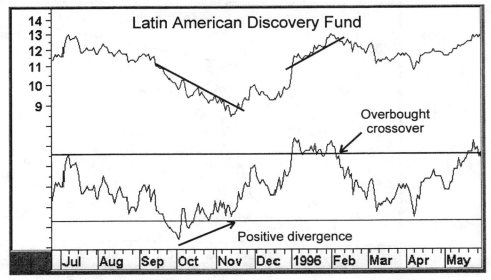

CHART 9-17. *Latin American Discovery Fund.*

judgment in these matters and wait for a more decisive penetration.

Chart 9-18 shows a linear uptrend in McDonalds. That's a trend that moves in a more or less steady, straight line and is interrupted, not by declines, but by temporary consolidations. Since this was a bull market for McDonalds, overbought readings in the 14-day RSI were not followed by declines. As you can see, the price never fell to an oversold condition during the course of the rally. This is a definite bull market characteristic and shows that you must also look at the longer-term indicators in order to gain some perspective on the primary or main trend. In short, don't expect overbought readings in a bull market to be followed by sharp declines, and don't expect oversold conditions in a bear market to be followed by worthwhile rallies.

The RSI occasionally throws up some price patterns. We see two examples in Chart 9-19. The October–November one is an upward-sloping head-and-shoulders top. This pattern is soon confirmed by a price trend break, but the price then consolidates rather than declines.

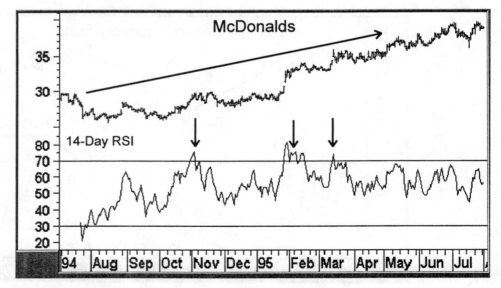

CHART 9-18.   *McDonalds.*

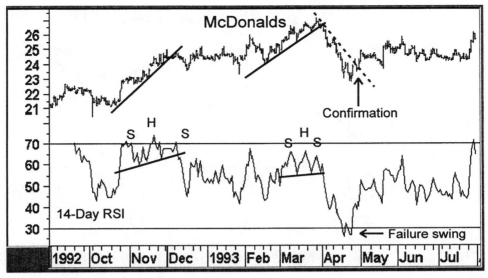

CHART 9-19. *McDonalds.*

Another head-and-shoulders formed in February–April 1993. This time, the trend break in the price was followed by a price decline. It did not last too long, and was terminated with a failure swing. See how the RSI first breaks below the oversold level, then crosses back above it. Then another test of the low and a rally above the previous top triggers the failure swing signal. This is later followed by a trend break in the price.

One final point. In the entire 11-month period covered, only one oversold condition is registered. The RSI does not spend much time there, because it is a bull market, and in a bull market more time is spent on the overbought side.

Chart 9-20 features a 26-week RSI of the Dow Jones Transports. Please note that because of the fairly lengthy time span, I have narrowed the overbought and oversold zones to 65 and 35. The point of the chart is to demonstrate that when the RSI moves to an extreme level and reverses direction, a change in the prevailing trend is likely. It is important, though, to wait for a trend confirmation in the price itself. On the left-hand side of the chart we see the RSI cross through the over-

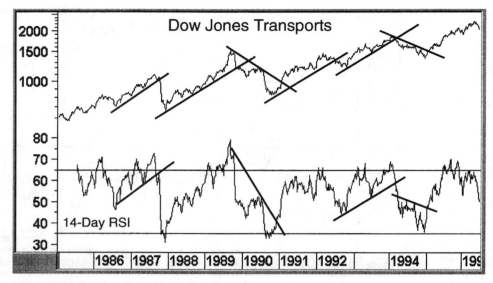

CHART 9-20.   *Dow Jones Transports.*

bought level a couple of times, without a meaningful price decline. It is only when the trendline in the price is penetrated that a decline materializes.

The oversold reading from the 1987 crash was associated with a major bottom, but there unfortunately was nothing which could serve as confirmation from price.

A similar situation to the 1987 crash sell signal also occurred in 1989, whereby several false overbought signals were eventually confirmed by a price trendline break. There was also a trend break in the RSI.

The next buy signal developed in late 1990, with a joint trend break, although the lines were not that significant, having been touched only twice each.

MOVING-AVERAGE CONVERGENCE DIVERGENCE (MACD)

So far we have limited our discussion to indicators that are essentially constructed by comparing the current price with a previous one. Another possibility is to relate the current price to some form of trend measurement. The assumption is that while prices move in trends they do not move in a straight line, but rather fluctuate around that trend. It is these fluctuations that form the basis for the calculation of momentum oscillators.

Because this type of calculation can result in some pretty jagged lines, the moving-average convergence divergence (MACD) calculation method—or "MacD," as it is sometimes known—is calculated by comparing two moving averages. The system gets its name from the fact that the two moving averages used in the calculation are continually converging and diverging from each other. Most people use exponential moving averages (EMAs) in the MACD calculation, the default being 12 for the shorter term and 26 for the longer average.

The top panel in Chart 9-21 shows the gold price together with a 12- and 26-day EMA. The middle panel reflects the relationship between the two averages and the lower panel, the oscillator derived from the division of the 12- by the 26-day average. The zero line represents those periods when the

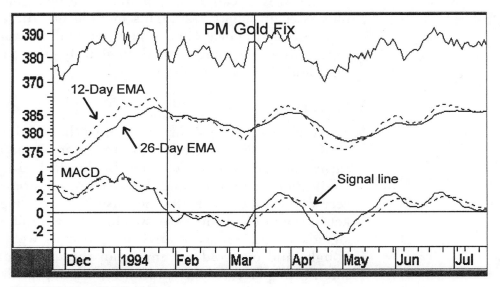

CHART 9-21. *PM Gold Fix.*

two EMAs are identical. When the MACD is above the equilibrium line, the shorter average is above the longer—and vice versa. The bottom panel also contains a third average, that's the dashed line. This is a 15-day EMA of the MACD, and is known as the signal line. It gets its name because signal-line crossovers of the MACD generate buy and sell signals.

My own experience has shown that these crossovers generate too many whipsaws. I therefore prefer to use the MACD from the point of view of trendline violations, divergences, or even price pattern construction.

Obviously, MACDs can be constructed from many different combinations. Gerald Appel of Signalert has done a substantial amount of work on the indicator and is arguably its chief proponent. He recommends a combination of 8-, 17-, and 9-day EMAs, but feels that sell signals are more reliable using a 12-, 25-, and 9-day combination. This is interesting because the "selling" MACD contains a longer time span. It reflects the point made in an earlier chapter, that markets spend more time in a rising than falling mode. The longer time span therefore has the effect of delaying the sell indications so they will be more timely.

The MACD can also be plotted in a histogram format, as illustrated in Chart 9-22. This method has the advantage of emphasizing the peaks and troughs but suffers from the disadvantage that it is more difficult to identify price pattern formations and trendline violations.

EXAMPLES

The vertical lines in Chart 9-23 show those points where the MACD reaches the overbought and oversold areas and then turns back toward the zero level. The dashed lines demonstrate short-term peaks and the solid ones bottoms. They work very well during this period because it is a trading-range market. If the price of this stock was in a more trending mode, the signals would not work anywhere near as well. Such overbought and oversold extremes can therefore be used as an intelligent place to take profits for trading positions, rather than as actual buy and sell signals unconfirmed by price.

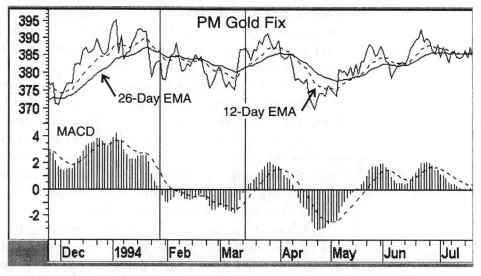

CHART 9-22. *PM Gold Fix.*

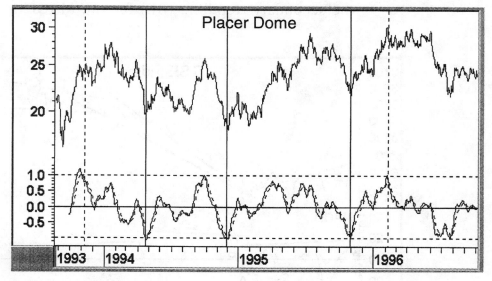

CHART 9-23. *Placer Dome.*

Note that the dashed line is the signal line. At first glance the signals appear to work well. However, if you examine the chart more closely, you can see that either the signals or crossovers turn out to be whipsaws or the trends following the signals are of too small a duration to result in any worthwhile price moves. Some of the signals, such as the one in April 1994, are followed by good rallies. And the one in November 1994 is followed by a reasonable decline, but by and large there are so many false signals that it is difficult to make any profit. Such action is fairly typical of most securities I have followed. In my experience trendline violations, divergences, and price pattern completions usually offer the best MACD results.

In Chart 9-24, of the FTSE Index, we see a trendline violation of the dashed line for both the price and the MACD. However, this very promising combination turns out to be a bit of a whipsaw, since the price immediately rallies and then falls back and marginally violates the extended line at A. The same is true for the momentum trendline. This is really the last bastion of support for the price. Fortunately, it passes the test. The MACD also traces out a series of rising bottoms, so when the secondary trendline (BB) for the MACD is violated, a

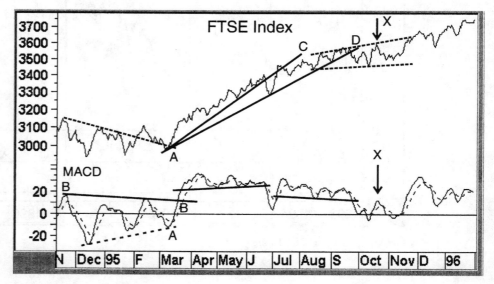

CHART 9-24. *FTSE Index.*

stronger buy signal results. Since the price remains above the original trendline, there is no need to wait for a confirmation, since the positive signal remains in force.

I chose this chart mainly to demonstrate how a perfectly legitimate signal using the principles discussed does not always work out. It's important to be aware of the fact that good signals do not always generate worthwhile moves. Please remember that these false signals are not singled out for the MACD. They develop with any indicator used in technical analysis.

Looking at the MACD in June of 1995, you can see that it broke down from a perfectly legitimate top formation. On the basis of this activity, it would have been perfectly correct to anticipate a decline once line AC had been violated. Instead, we got a small decline, after which the price rallied to a new high. Then another top, which diverged negatively from the first, was completed and a valid trendline for the price (AD) was penetrated. This was an even better sell signal than the first, especially as the FTSE then rallied to a new marginal high, on virtually no momentum, at point X.

The two dashed lines suggest the formation of a broadening top with an almost flat bottom. What should then happen is for the price to break below the lower line and for a sharp decline to follow. However, you can see that the price did not break down, but rallied quite nicely.

This kind of action is, unfortunately, typical of markets in a strong trend—in this case, an uptrend. Had you gone short on the basis of this weak-looking technical structure, the best thing to have done would be to cover immediately when the price made a new high at this point. The decision to go short was based on certain criteria. When the market did not respond in the expected way, it was time to liquidate the position and look for another promising situation.

STOCHASTICS

The stochastic (probabilistic) indicator gained a lot of popularity in the 1980s, probably because of its simple, deliberate style which, on the face of it, appears to offer profitable and easy-to-follow signals (Chart 9-25). The stochastics concept rests on the assumption that prices tend to close near the upper part of the trading range during an uptrend and near the lower part during a downtrend. The range in this instance refers to the trading period under consideration. For example, daily data would embrace a trading range for the day, weekly for the week, and so forth. As the trend approaches a turning point, the price closes further away from the extreme. Figure 9-8 shows an uptrend. Note how the horizontal bars, representing the closing price, develop close to the high at the start of the uptrend. However, as the trend matures, the closing price develops closer to the low of the day. The objective of the stochastics formula therefore, is to try to identify those points in an advancing market when the closes are clustered nearer to the lows than the highs, since this indicates that a trend reversal is at hand. For down markets the process is reversed.

The stochastic indicator is displayed in Figure 9-9 in the form of two lines, known as percent D and percent K. The %K is the more sensitive of the two, but it is the %D line which carries the greater weight and gives the major signals. I always

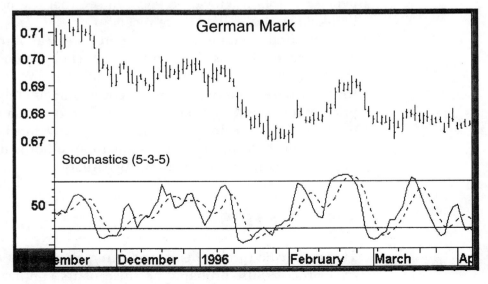

CHART 9-25. *German mark.*

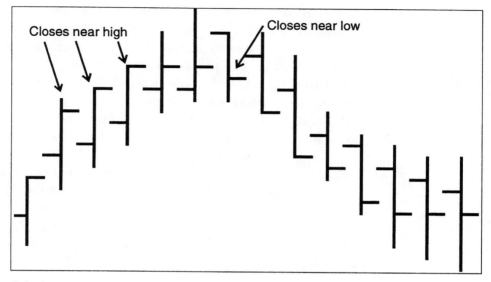

FIGURE 9-8.

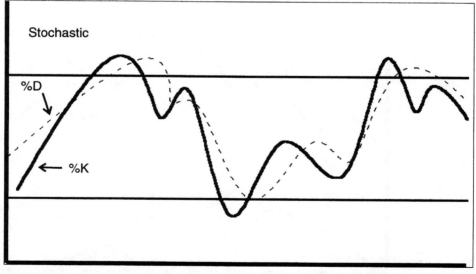

FIGURE 9-9.

get confused between the two, but a simple reminder is to think of K as standing for Kwick and D for Dawdling.

The *slow stochastic* is a smoothed variation of the regular series. In this calculation, the original %K line is eliminated and the old %D substituted for it. This renamed or "slowed" %K is then averaged by 3 days to form the "%D slow." Since the regular formula is more likely to be subject to whipsaws, I will be using the slowed version in this presentation.

The %K is usually plotted as a solid line and its slower %D counterpart is expressed as a dashed or dotted line. I often have trouble remembering which line is which. The stochastic indicator always falls in the range of 0 to 100. A reading near 80 is generally regarded as overbought and 20 as oversold. These are the default lines that most charting packages and chart services use.

INTERPRETATION

1. *Divergences* (Figure 9-10).   Divergences between the %D and the price are similar to those discussed in the previous chapter. The principal difference between stochastic and RSI

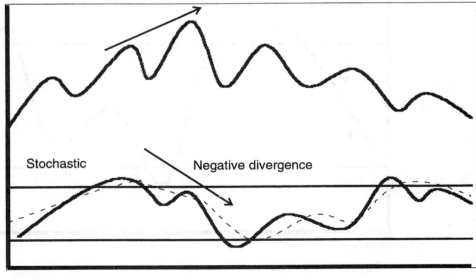

FIGURE 9-10.

divergences is that there are usually fewer of them. In fact, it is probably true to say that in the vast majority of cases the %D experiences only one, or at the most two, divergences.

2. *Crossovers* (Figure 9-11). Normally the more sensitive Kwick or %K will turn and cross the Dawdling or slower %D before the D changes direction. See how K crosses below D before D peaks. This is normal because K, being Kwick, is more sensitive. According to George Lane, the inventor of the indicator, the strongest stochastics signal comes when the %K crosses from the right-hand side of the peak in the %D line (i.e., K crosses D *after* D changes direction). Where the arrow shows the peak in D, now see how K crosses D after D peaks. You can see that buy signals are triggered when the %K crosses the right-hand side of low point of the %D line at bottoms. Lane emphasizes that these right-hand crossovers are more reliable.

3. *The hinge* (Figure 9-12). The hinge is a slowing down in the velocity of either line. This implies a reversal in the next trading period (next day for daily data, week for weekly data,

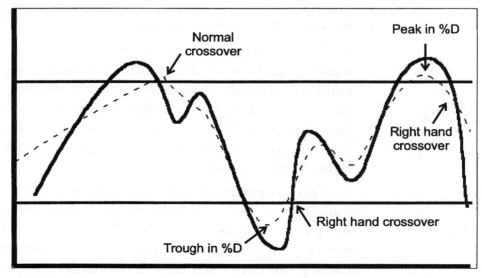

FIGURE 9-11.

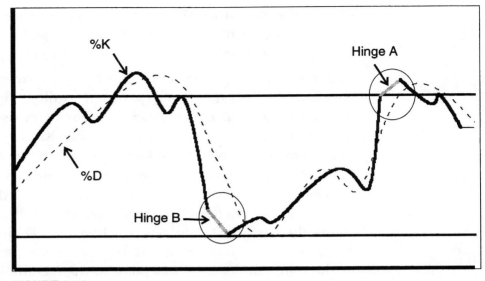

FIGURE 9-12.

and so forth). See how the line, and here we are talking about %K, rallies sharply on the left, then upside momentum dissipates as the ascent of %K becomes noticeably less pronounced—that's the period after the arrow. Example B shows the same characteristics for a bottom.

4. *Warning* (Figure 9-13).   In the case of a rising market, a warning occurs when the %K line has been rising for a while and then one day (or week or month, depending on the time frame being used) reverses sharply. This represents a warning that only one or two more days of rising movement are likely prior to a reversal in trend. The opposite, as shown on the right, is true in a declining market.

5. *%K reaching an extreme* (Figure 9-14).   Normally when an indicator reaches an overbought or oversold extreme, a possible trend reversal is signaled. However, when the %K line moves to the extreme of 0 percent or 100 percent, this indicates pronounced strength or weakness. In the case of an

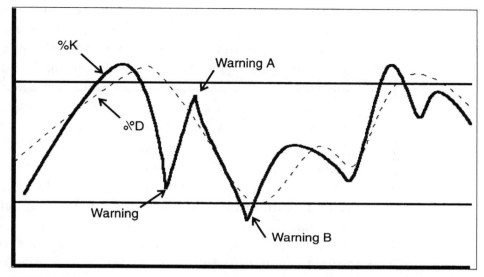

FIGURE 9-13.

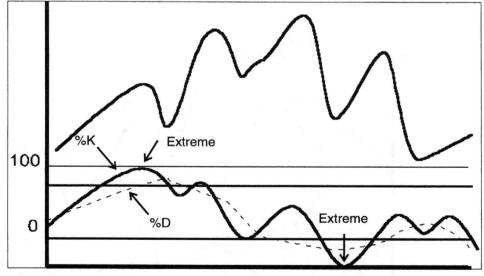

FIGURE 9-14.

overbought situation, a move to 100 percent, or very close to it, indicates that once the overbought condition has been worked off, the next rally is likely to take the price higher, as in Figure 9-14. Typically the %K will retreat 20% to 25% from the 100% level, later rallying back toward it again. It is when this testing process is under way that the actual price should work its way to new high ground.

The opposite is true of falling markets in relation to the 0 percent extreme. First expect a rally, then a reaction to new lows. While these extreme readings are, on the one hand, telling us that things are overdone for the time being, the very fact that the stochastic has been able to reach it indicates an underlying strength. Once the correction has run its course, expect a new high following a 100 percent reading, or a new low for a 0 percent reading.

6. *Failure* (Figure 9-15). At market bottoms, failure occurs when the %K line crosses above the %D and then falls back for a couple of days but manages to remain above the %D line. It represents a kind of test that, if successful, indicates that

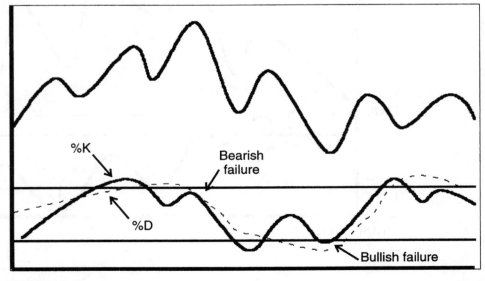

FIGURE 9-15.

the new uptrend is likely to continue. On the right, you see the same concept for a market top. See how the K line crosses above the D, then falls back, successfully holds above %D, and then goes on to recover to a new high. This type of action is very similar to the failure swing for the RSI, considered earlier in this chapter.

EXAMPLES

Chart 9-26 is constructed from a 5-3-5—that is, a %K smoothed with a 5-day average, a slowing factor of 3, and a %D with a 5-day average. It happens to be the default (i.e., standard time span) for the MetaStock™ charting package. In mid-July we can see a good example of a failure. See how the %K crosses below %D and then tries to rally back above it, but just fails to do so. Then, in mid-April, we see a hinge. The stochastic is falling quite sharply, then downside momentum begins to dissipate, and it reverses to the upside. Another bullish hinge develops in mid-June at the bottom.

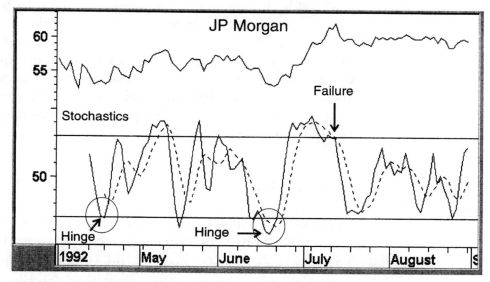

CHART 9-26. *J. P. Morgan.*

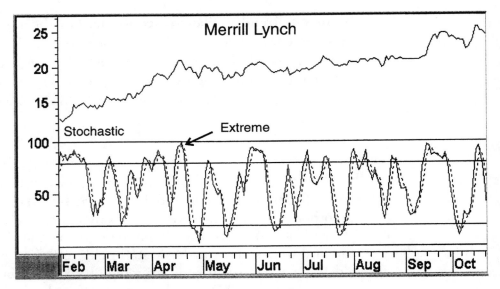

CHART 9-27. *Merrill Lynch.*

Chart 9-27 shows a *stochastics extreme,* with the indicator rallying to the 100 extreme level. Normally an overbought reading is a signal of impending weakness. In this case, the extreme reading does signal short-term weakness. However, usually after the stochastic has reached an extreme level on the upside, higher prices are ultimately seen. In this case the extreme reading is a sign of a very strong market.

This chart also shows a number of crossovers. The best ones seem to come when the %K crosses above or below %D or very close to the overbought and oversold zones. Generally speaking, I do not find the stochastic to offer such good signals as the trendline and price pattern analysis associated with the ROC and RSI.

SUMMARY

1. Rate of change is a simple concept to measure the acceleration or deceleration of a price trend over time.

2. ROC can be calculated for any time frame and is subject to all the principles of interpretation described in the pre-

vious chapter, especially trendline and price pattern construction.

3. The principal disadvantage of the ROC is that it does not provide predefined levels that can be used for the construction of overbought and oversold lines.

4. The RSI is an oscillator whose construction confines it within a band bounded by 100 on the upside and 0 on the downside.

5. The RSI's strength lies in overbought/oversold and divergence analysis.

6. The MACD is an oscillator constructed from the relationship of two moving averages.

7. The MACD is best used with a signal line, trendline violations, and divergence analysis.

8. The stochastic method assumes that as a trend matures, prices tend to close further from a trading session high in a rising market and low in a declining one.

9. The stochastic consists of two lines: a sensitive %K and a slower moving %D.

10. The principal uses of the stochastic are crossovers and divergences.

HOW TO MAKE VOLUME WORK FOR YOU

INTRODUCTION

Almost every indicator we have looked at so far has been constructed from a statistical manipulation of price alone. This means that each of these indicators represents a variation on a theme. Volume, on the other hand, not only monitors the enthusiasm of buyers and sellers but is a totally independent variable from price. It is therefore a very useful addition to the technical arsenal. I mentioned earlier that it is *mandatory* to use the weight of the evidence when attempting to identify market turning points. Using volume in the analysis is one way in which we can get some new evidence from an entirely different dimension than price-manipulated statistics. Volume offers independent evidence of price trend reversals!

Two benefits are obtained. First, when we look at indicators which measure both price and volume momentum, it is possible to see whether they are in agreement. If they are, it increases the odds that any trend reversal signals will be reliable. Second, when indicators disagree, it warns us of an underlying weakness in the prevailing trend. In this way an advance notice of a potential trend reversal is given.

Volume is usually represented as a series of histograms appearing just under the price series itself (Figure 10-1). This arrangement is generally acceptable, since it highlights significant expansions and contractions in trading activity. These in turn confirm or question the sustainability of the price trend

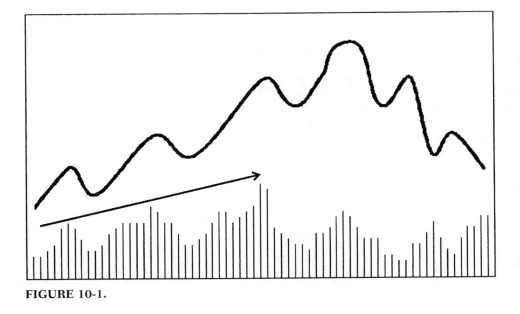

FIGURE 10-1.

itself. Volume may also be expressed in a momentum format, which has the effect of accentuating fluctuations in volume levels in a more graphic way. These are covered in the advanced CD-ROM course on technical analysis. Therefore, we will confine ourselves here to the basic principles concerning the relationship between price and volume.

PRINCIPLES OF VOLUME INTERPRETATION

1. The most important principle is that *volume normally goes with the trend*. In a rising market, volume should be expanding and in a declining market it should contract. Rising volume refers to the average daily, weekly, or monthly transaction level relative to itself. Prices move in trends, but do not generally rise and fall in a straight line as reactions to the prevailing trend set in. The same principle applies to volume.

In the left side of Figure 10-1, for instance, the arrow shows that the volume trend is up. By the same token, it is apparent that the level of activity does not expand every day. There are quiet days and there are active ones, but the general thrust is up. In the right-hand part of the diagram the trend is down, but irregularly so. When we talk of rising or contracting volume, we are therefore referring to the trend. Volume trends, like those of price, can be of short, intermediate, or long duration.

Activity should always be measured in relation to the recent past; otherwise it has little meaning. For example, the number of stocks listed on the NYSE in the 1990s was far greater than at the beginning of the century. The increase in volume resulting from an expansion in the number of listed companies and arbitrage activity in futures and options, therefore, has no significance when making volume comparisons over long periods.

An important factor to bear in mind is that volume reflects an exchange between buyers and sellers. By definition, the money flowing into the market must always equal the money flowing out. This is true whether volume is heavy or light. It is the relative enthusiasm of buyers to sellers that determines the direction of prices. Heavy volume accompanied by rising prices implies that a substantial amount of selling is being absorbed. This means there is likely to be less overhead resistance as prices climb further.

2. Rising volume and price are a normal phenomenon. This combination indicates that the market is "in gear." It has no forecasting value, except to expect the final top in prices to be preceded by a volume peak. Consequently, if the two are in gear, it is reasonable to expect at least one more rally that reaches a new price high where they are not.

3. Volume normally leads price. A new high in price that is not confirmed by volume should be regarded as a red flag, warning that the prevailing trend may be about to reverse. In

Figure 10-2 the price peaks at point C, yet volume reached its maximum at point A. Such action is normal, the lower-volume peaks warning of impending trouble for the price. There are no hard-and-fast rules about how many divergences precede a peak in price, but generally speaking the lower the diverging peaks become in relation to the earlier ones, the greater the danger. A new high accompanied by virtually no volume is just as bearish in its implications as a new high that is registered with virtually no upside momentum.

4. Rising prices and falling volume are abnormal, and indicate a weak and suspect rally (Figure 10-3). Volume measures the enthusiasm of buyers relative to sellers. Consequently, rising prices and declining volume indicate the market is rallying because of lack of selling pressure, not because buyers are enthusiastic. Sooner or later the market will reach a price level that stimulates selling. Afterward, prices typically fall substantially. This characteristic of short-term rallies and declining or weak volume is typical during a primary bear market.

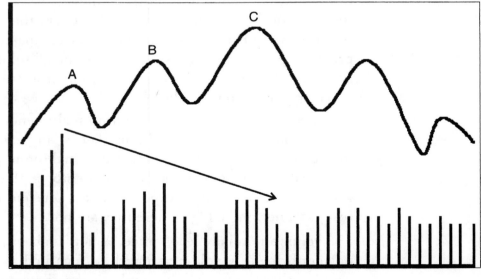

FIGURE 10-2.

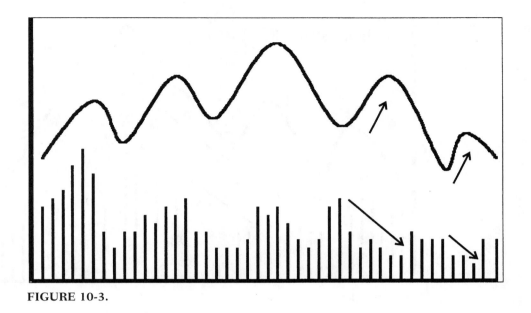

FIGURE 10-3.

5. A parabolic rise in prices and a sharp increase in volume are unsustainable, and eventually result in an exhaustion move (Figure 10-4). Exhaustion is characteristic of an important market turning point. Its significance will depend on the nature of the buying frenzy relative to the time over which it occurred. A buying panic spread over 4 or 5 days will have far less significance than one which gradually builds up over, say, a 6-week period. Unfortunately, exhaustion or blow-off moves such as this are not easy to define in the sense that it is possible to construct clearly definable lines as we do for rectangle patterns. For that reason, it is not usually possible to spot the terminal phase until a day or so after volume and price have reached their crescendo.

6. The reverse set of circumstances, when the price declines sharply and volume expands to climactic levels, is a selling climax (Figure 10-5). The implications and principles for a buying panic hold for a selling climax, but in this case the trend reverses from down to up. Selling climaxes normally, but not

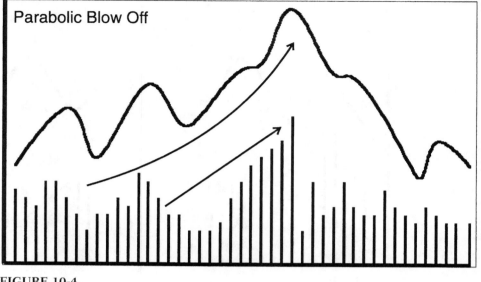

FIGURE 10-4.

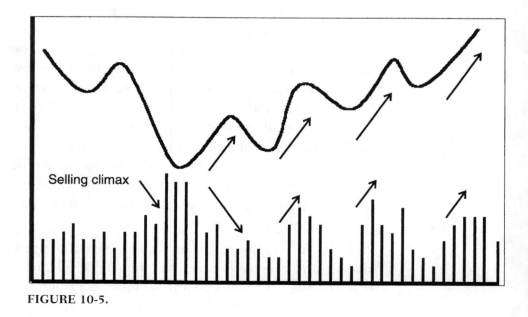

FIGURE 10-5.

always, represent the final low of a declining price trend. By definition, the rise in price following a selling climax is accompanied by declining volume. This is one of the few times when a volume and price divergence is normal. With that said, it is still of paramount importance that subsequent rallies are accompanied by expanding volume. A selling climax involves liquidation by most all the "weak" holders. As a result, any additional bad news will be unlikely to attract significant amounts of selling. Consequently, a market that can take bearish news in its stride indicates a strong technical position.

7. When a test of an important low is accompanied by lower volume, this is a bullish sign (Figure 10-6). It is not important whether the first low is marginally violated by the second or if the second low holds just above the first. There is an old saying on Wall Street: "Never short a dull market." It applies very much to this type of situation, in which a previous low is being tested. The almost nonexistent volume indicates a complete lack of selling interest.

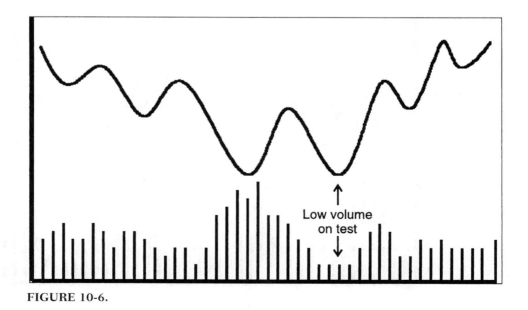

FIGURE 10-6.

8. Expanding volume, when prices are falling, is bearish because volume is not going with the trend. An expansion of volume following a price peak, during a consolidation, or accompanying a downward price pattern completion is a bearish sign, since it indicates that volume is not going with the trend (Figure 10-7).

9. After the price has been in a rallying phase for *some time* and additional increases are anemic and accompanied by heavy volume, churning activity is taking place. It is a bearish sign (Figure 10-8). The definition of *some time* will depend on the nature of the price trend under consideration.

10. Stable prices and abnormally heavy volume following a decline represents accumulation, which is bullish. If, after a lengthy decline, prices stabilize and volume expands to abnormal proportions, it is indicative of accumulation. This is a bullish sign. If the price subsequently breaks out on the upside accompanied by even higher volume, this is an extremely positive sign (Figure 10-9).

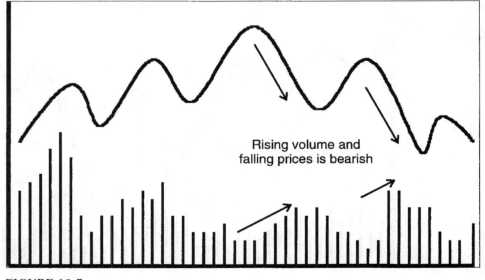

Rising volume and
falling prices is bearish

FIGURE 10-7.

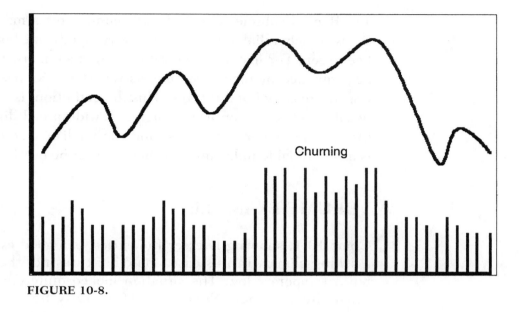

FIGURE 10-8.

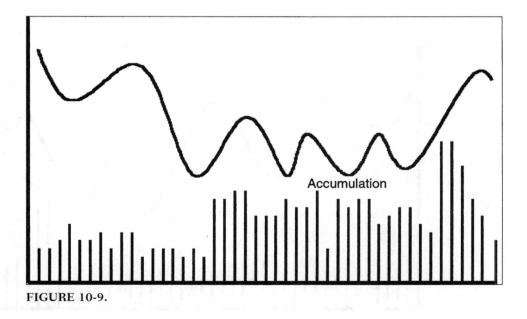

FIGURE 10-9.

11. Record volume (Figure 10-10) coming off a major low is an extremely reliable signal that a very significant bottom has been seen. For instance, the 1982 U.S. stock market low was accompanied by record volume, as was the 1987 bear market low in Treasury bond futures. This, by definition, is a very unusual event. One confirming sign is a widespread disbelief in the rally by traders, investors, and the media. Record volume is a very reliable indicator and should never be overlooked.

VOLUME EXAMPLES

Chart 10-1, showing Dresser Industries, is a good example of a selling climax. In this case, the climax was not the bottom, but a temporary low. The situation looked quite encouraging until the October–November 1994 rally began. This is because the price rose on declining volume. Volume was not moving in sympathy with the trend—a bearish factor—and, not surprisingly, prices began to slip again.

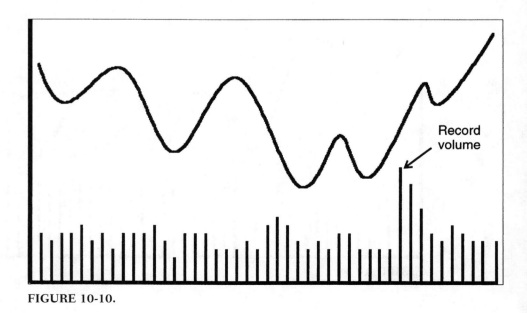

FIGURE 10-10.

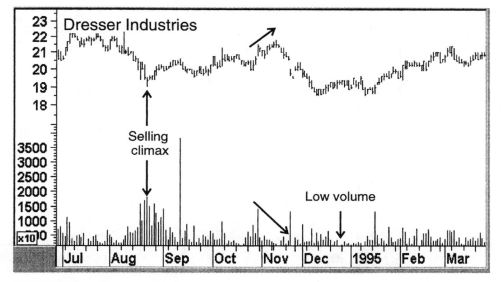

CHART 10-1. *Dresser Industries.*

On a more positive note, you can see that the final low, formed in December 1994 and January 1995, was associated with very light volume in comparison with the selling climax that had taken place earlier.

The Turkish Fund (Chart 10-2), a closed-end investment fund listed on the NYSE, was in a bear market for most of 1994. To the casual observer, it may have appeared that the sharp sell-off in the spring of 1994 was sufficient to turn the trend. However, any hopes of this would have been dashed in April, since the rally took place on a trend of falling volume. Unfortunately, this is a bear market characteristic and, true to form, prices declined to a new low.

In Chart 10-3, of the Thai Capital Fund, we see a parabolic blow-off as both prices and volume expand to previously unheard of levels. These formations are extremely difficult to detect while they are developing, because it is not possible to determine when the exhaustion move will run its course. However, as the parabola begins to form and prices really begin to accelerate, it is fairly evident that the rally is unlikely

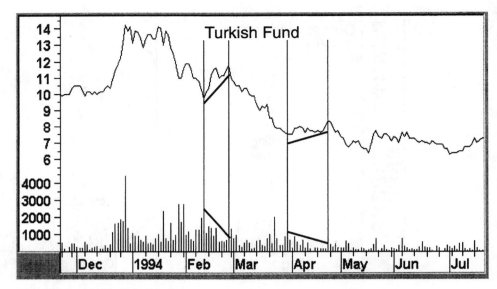

CHART 10-2. *Turkish Fund.*

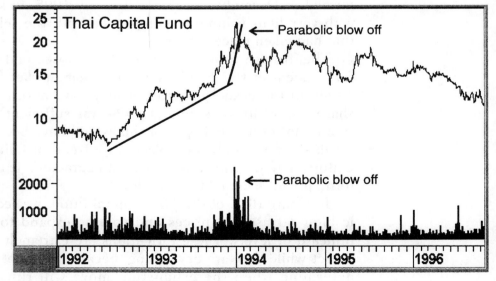

CHART 10-3. *Thai Capital Fund.*

to continue for much longer. When a security becomes so unstable, it is usually a good idea to forget the icing and just take the cake.

SUMMARY

1. Volume levels should always be compared with the recent past.
2. It is normal for volume to go with the trend.
3. When volume goes against the direction of the trend, it is warning of a probable trend reversal.

INTRODUCTION TO CANDLESTICK CHARTING

Candle charts have been in use in Japan for several centuries, but have only recently been adopted as a legitimate tool in the West. This technique has now become very popular, especially among traders. Since the charts reflect short-term phenomena, their forecasting abilities are also short term—rarely lasting more than 10 days and often much less. There are numerous ways in which to interpret this interesting technique, but in an introductory presentation such as this, we must limit ourselves to the most widely followed and useful price formations.

BASICS OF CANDLE CONSTRUCTION

The information displayed in candlestick charts is identical to that of bar charts (Figure 11-1). Each method contains the opening, high, low, and closing prices. It is the way in which candlesticks are displayed that makes them unique and gives them special interpretive powers. When I talk of prices, I am referring to a particular time period, such as a day, week, or month. While they can be plotted for any period, candlesticks are almost always used with daily data, which is what we will use here. Please remember that most candlesticks are very short-term phenomena, so their implications as to future price activity is normally limited to fewer than 10 trading days, often less. For this reason, candlesticks are best used for trading purposes.

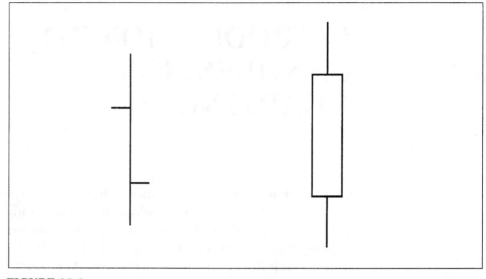

FIGURE 11-1.

Bar charts treat the opening, closing, high, and low prices
more or less equally. The candlestick method places special
emphasis on the opening and closing prices. How people feel
about a security when they start the trading day and their attitude toward it when the session closes are therefore of paramount importance to candlestick enthusiasts. Opening and
closing prices are represented in the chart by a rectangle, such
as that in Figure 11-2. The top of the rectangle represents the
higher of the two prices, and the bottom the lower. For example, if the close was $10 and the opening was $9.50, the top
part of the rectangle would be plotted at $10 and the lower
part at $9.50. You may be asking: "How can we tell which is
the opening and which is the closing?" The answer lies in the
color of the rectangle. If it is white or empty, as in the example
on the extreme left, the lower part of the rectangle represents
the opening, and the top part represents the closing price. On
the other hand, if the rectangle is black or filled in, the opening price is at the top and the closing at the bottom. Normally
we like to see the price rise during the day, so the black or

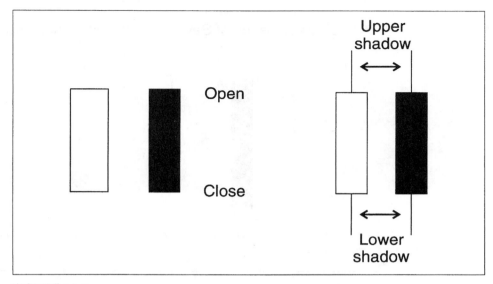

FIGURE 11-2.

dark aspect of the rectangle offers a kind of bearish overtone. In technical jargon this rectangle is referred to as the *real body.*

When I first looked at candles, I quickly assumed that black candles meant down days and white candles were up days. That of course is not true, since it is possible for a black candle to close above yesterday's close, or even above yesterday's high. What makes a candle black is the fact that the close plotted at the bottom of the real body is always below the open, which is plotted at the top. For white candles, the open is at the bottom and the close at the top. But what of the high and the low for the day? These are represented by thin lines that appear above and below the real body. These lines are known as *shadows.* The line above the real body is the upper shadow and the one below it the lower shadow.

Since the four pieces of data that go into the construction of a candle can fluctuate considerably, there are numerous variations in the way in which they are plotted. Some possibilities are shown in Figure 11-3. If the opening and closing prices

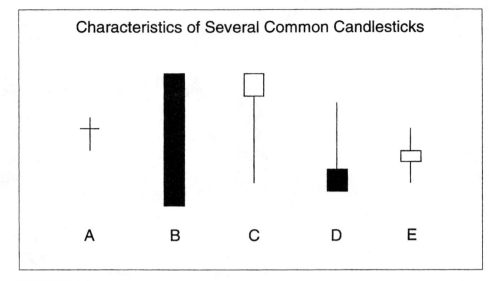

Characteristics of Several Common Candlesticks

A   B   C   D   E

FIGURE 11-3.

are identical, the real body will appear as a horizontal line (A). If they represent the high and low of the day, there will be no shadows (B). It is possible that the opening and closing prices are near the high of the day (C) or the low of the day (D). Finally, the day's trading range may be very small (E).

Some of these extreme examples have special names and can have forecasting characteristics in their own right, just as bar charts have outside days, key reversal days, and so forth. For instance, a candle in which the opening and closing prices are very close to the low and high, respectively, and the range between the open and close is large is called a long white line (A in Figure 11-4). The opposite, when the close is near the low and the open near the high is known as a long black line (B). In order to qualify as a long black line, the candle must have a relatively large range between the opening and the closing. As mentioned earlier, long white lines tend to be bull- ish and long black lines bearish. We shall see later that these variations often form part of price patterns, in the same way as

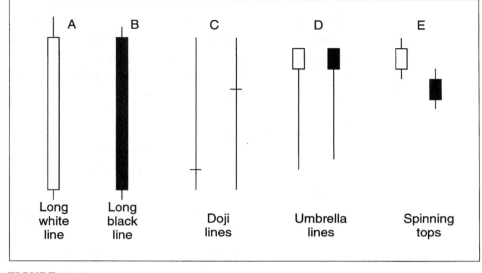

FIGURE 11-4.

bars in a bar chart. The principal difference is that candle patterns are usually very short term and therefore take a much briefer time to complete. What constitutes a long line can be determined only with reference to the other candles that have appeared in the recent past. For example, what may be considered a long day in a very quiet and subdued market may be far less "long" than that in a very volatile period, when a typical trading range for a day is much greater.

When the opening and closing prices are the same, or very close to it, candles are known as Doji lines (C). Their interpretation depends on the context in which they appear. With umbrella lines (D), the opening and closing prices develop close to the high of the day. The real body in this case more closely resembles a square than a rectangle. Umbrellas tend to be bullish after a decline and bearish following an advance. If they develop during trading ranges, they have no significance.

Finally, spinning tops (E) are characterized by very narrow real bodies, in which the shadows are wider. It is the size of the real body rather than that of the shadows which is important in identifying a spinning top. Spinning tops are not important when they appear in trading ranges, but they do have some significance when they develop in price patterns, some of which we will consider later.

Since these terms are probably very new to you, I'll quickly review them before we proceed:

1. Long white lines (A) occur when the closing is above the opening price and they are far apart.
2. With long black lines (B), the close is below the open and they are far apart.
3. When the opening and closing prices are almost identical, we have a doji (C).
4. Umbrellas occur when the real body is narrow and close to the day's high (D).
5. The spinning top (E) can be identified as a narrow real body in a day with a narrow trading range. The shadows are usually wider than the real body.

Now that we have covered the building blocks, it is time to review some of the chart patterns. With candles, as with bar charts, there are two types of patterns or formations: reversal, and continuation. We'll start with the reversal variety.

REVERSAL PATTERNS

HAMMERS AND HANGING MAN

Hammers and hanging men (Figure 11-5) are 1-day price reversals. Hammers are umbrellas occurring after a price decline and get their name because they are "hammering" out a bottom. A hammer is characterized by a day in which prices slip sharply from the opening price during the course of the trading session, then return close to the high of the day. Hanging men, on the other hand, are umbrellas that develop after a rally. In a sense, the small real body can be compared

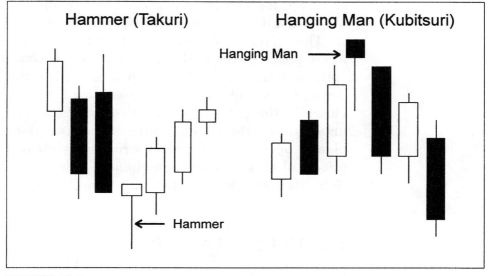

FIGURE 11-5.

with the head of a man, and the long shadow, with his legs dangling down. The shadow should be at least twice the size of the real body. Hanging men that develop after a prolonged advance should be treated with great respect, especially if the trading range for the "hanging" day is above the entire trading range of the previous day. In bar chart language, the hanging day would be a gap day. The color of either the hanging men or the hammers is not important.

DARK CLOUD COVER AND THE PIERCING LINE

As we all know, dark clouds hint at a coming storm. The dark cloud candlestick formation (Figure 11-6) does the same thing, but for prices. The pattern consists of 2 days which follow an advance. The first is a strong real white body. The second is a black body in which the close occurs in the lower half of the first day's white real body. It is also important for the second day's opening to be higher than that of the first day. You can tell that by making sure that the top of the real body is above the first day's upper shadow line. Generally speaking, the lower the close on the second day, relative to the real body of the first day, the more bearish the pattern.

The piercing line occurs at market bottoms and is exactly the opposite of the dark cloud. For this reason, it could more aptly be termed a sunny sky. In Figure 11-6, the first day is a strong black real body, and the second a white real body that closes in the top half of the first day's real body. Again it is important for the opening price of the second day to gap completely beyond the first day's real body. Also, the more the price can close above the midpoint, as in the example on the right, the more positive the implication.

ENGULFING PATTERNS

Engulfing patterns (Figure 11-7) are 2-day affairs. A bearish engulfing pattern develops after a rally. The first day consists of a long real white body, followed by a dark real body, whose opening price is higher than the first day's and whose closing

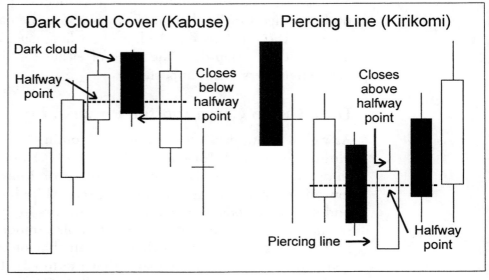

FIGURE 11-6.

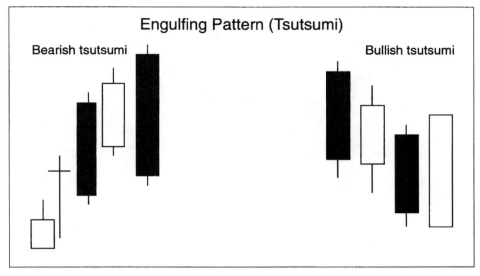

FIGURE 11-7.

price is also below the first day's. In effect, the second day's real body totally engulfs that of the first day. It is important to note that both days should be relatively shadowless.

A bullish engulfing pattern is the exact opposite of the bearish one. This pattern, which follows a decline, consists of a long black real body followed by a long white real body that engulfs the first day's body. It is the second day that gives us a clue as to the psychology underlying the pattern. In the case of a bearish real body, shown on the left, prices open higher as people expect the bullish action of the first day to continue. Then, as the session proceeds, the bulls lose their enthusiasm as prices close down on the day. This 1-day reversal of upside to downside momentum is sufficiently great to result in a changed sentiment of trend. Generally speaking, the longer the trend preceding the pattern, the greater its significance. For example, a bullish engulfing pattern that develops after a small price decline will have less validity than one following a more lengthy decline.

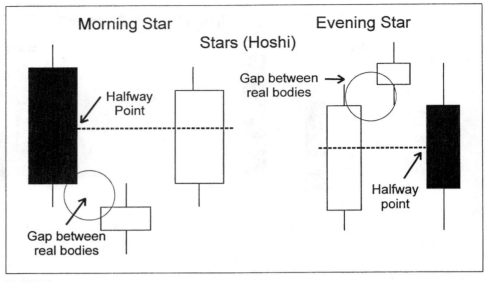

FIGURE 11-8.

STARS

Stars are a combination of long real bodies and spinning tops (Figure 11-8) and come in four principal varieties: morning, evening, doji, and shooting stars. Let's begin with the morning star. The morning star begins a new day of hope and is therefore bullish. These patterns are formed with two long real bodies separated by a spinning top. The actual star is the spinning top which, as you can see from the morning star example, is made with a gap. In this case the real body of the star falls outside the range of the other two real bodies, although, in some cases shadows do overlap. See how the real body of the spinning top falls completely outside of the trading range of the first day. The first real body should be black. The color of the second real body is important, and since this is a bullish pattern, it should be white. It should also close above the halfway point of the first real body.

The evening star signals a close to the rally, and is the reverse of the morning star. It too consists of 3 days. A long white body is separated from a black real body by a spinning top. The real body of the spinning top should ideally fall outside the real body of the other 2 days. Finally, the third day should close more than halfway below the midpoint of the first (i.e., below the horizontal line).

Technicians usually like to see a confirmation of the star. In the case of a top, this would take the form of a long black real body. If a long white real body follows, the odds are greater that the pattern will fail.

A doji star (Figure 11-9) consists of a long real body followed by a small doji. You may recall that a doji is a day in which the opening and closing prices are more or less identical. A doji star offers a warning that a trend is about to reverse. The long real body should be colored in the direction of the then-prevailing trend. In other words, if the prevailing trend is up, look for a white real body. If the prevailing trend is down, look for a dark real body for the first day. The doji should gap outside the first day's real body. Note that the trading range for the doji day is very small.

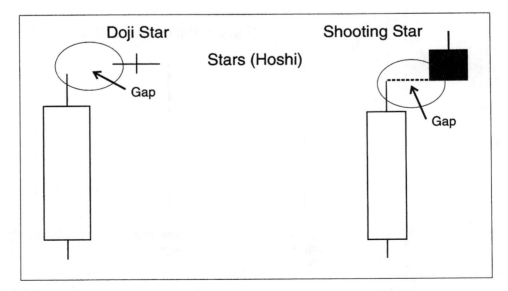

FIGURE 11-9.

Finally, we turn to the shooting star (Figure 11-9). This is a short-term top in which, after an advance, the price action creates a small gap and a small black real body appears at the end of a long wick or upper shadow.

MORE ON DOJIS

You may recall that a doji is a candle in which the opening and closing prices are more or less identical. This particular example (Figure 11-10) is known as a long-legged doji. In a way it indicates indecision, since prices fluctuate greatly throughout the day, as you can see from the long shadows. However, at the end of the day the price returns to its opening level. The long-legged doji therefore has no forecasting value.

On the other hand, the gravestone doji shows the opening and closing prices occurring at the low for the day, and is quite bearish. We typically see it at the end of an advance, where the upper shadow represents new high ground for the move. The fact that prices end the day at the opening, after all that work at higher levels, is indicative of a change in psychol-

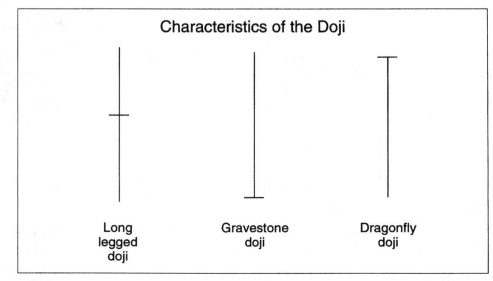

FIGURE 11-10.

ogy. In this case, the longer the shadow, the more negative the omen.

The dragonfly doji represents a more optimistic scenario. This is really a special case of the hammer that we looked at earlier. The psychology is the exact reverse of that of the gravestone doji. These candles should develop at the end of a decline. The price should open at the high, then sell off (the more the merrier in this case), finally rallying back to the opening levels at the high for the day.

UPSIDE GAP TWO CROWS

The pattern shown in Figure 11-11 occurs after a rally. It consists of a long real white body, which is then followed by two small black real bodies. The first black body gaps up from the white body. In other words, its price range is totally above that of the first day. This is where the "upside gap" in the name of the pattern comes from. The second black real body normally closes the gap; however, because it is a black day, the implication is bearish. Ideally, the real body of this third day of the

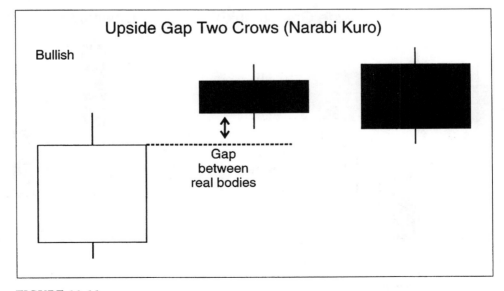

FIGURE 11-11.

pattern engulfs the second day, yet still closes above the close of the first day. The pattern gets its name from the idea that the black candlesticks represent two black crows looking down from a tree.

CONTINUATION PATTERNS

Continuation patterns occur within the confines of an uptrend or downtrend. They represent a couple of days or so of consolidation. Following the completion of the pattern, prices are expected to resume the prevailing trend. We will consider two continuation patterns.

UPSIDE GAP (TASUKI) AND DOWNSIDE GAP (TASUKI)

The upside gap is shown in Figure 11-12. It is formed during an advance when a white candlestick gaps up from another white candlestick. It is then followed by a black candlestick which opens within the previous day's real body and then

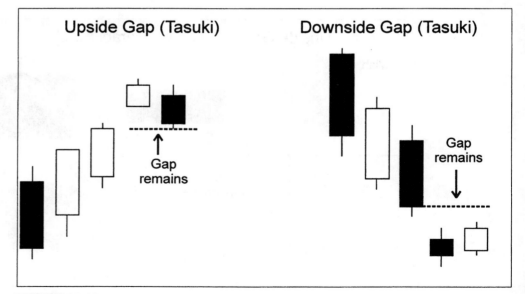

FIGURE 11-12.

closes below the previous day's open. However, to qualify as an upside gap, the black candlestick must leave the gap created by the second day intact.

The downside gap is the exact opposite. In this instance, a black candlestick is followed by another black one that gaps to the downside. Then a white candlestick opens within the black body of the second. It closes above the opening of the second candlestick, but does not close the gap. Once these patterns have been completed, the prevailing trend is expected to continue.

RISING-THREE METHODS AND FALLING-THREE METHODS

Figure 11-13 shows a bullish rising-three method. It consists of a long white candlestick formed in the direction of the prevailing trend. This is then followed by three or four declining small candles, ideally black in color. The important point is that the trading range for this series of declining lines remains within the high and low of the first strong white day. The pattern is completed with another strong white day in which the

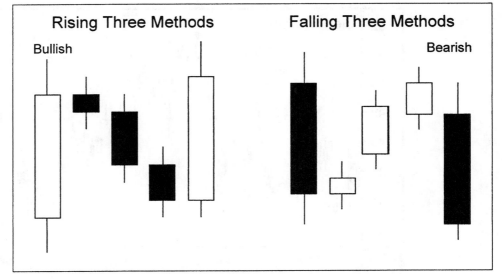

FIGURE 11-13.

price opens above the previous close and closes at a new high. It is important for volume to contract on the black days and expand noticeably on the final white day.

The falling-three methods occur during downtrends. It consists of 1 strong black day followed by 3 or 4 small rising days, ideally white in color. The final day should open under the previous day's close and close at a new low for the move.

EXAMPLES

Chart 11-1, of General Motors, shows a good example of a bearish engulfing pattern. Note that the two high points of the real bodies, the close for the white body and the open for the dark one, are identical. This still counts as an engulfing pattern, provided the low for the black day engulfs the opening for the white one, which it does. Had the size of both real bodies been identical, the pattern would not have counted as an engulfing formation.

As we move on, you can see that the decline did not last very long. This is not uncommon, because candlestick formations do not have a lasting effect on prices. A small rally

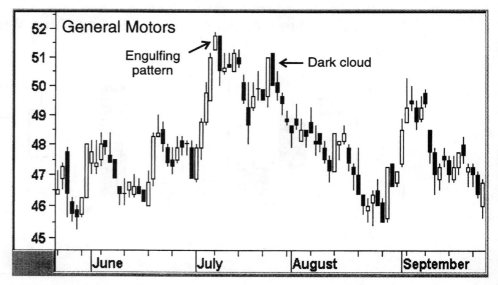

CHART 11-1. *General Motors.*

ensues, then we get a dark cloud formation. Remember the rules—after the market has been rallying, which it has, the first day should be a long white real body. Then the second day should be a black real body, which opens higher than the first day and closes below the midpoint of the first.

Chart 11-2 shows a series of engulfing patterns. I have used it to demonstrate how candlestick patterns can have very short-term forecasting implications. The first one (A) followed a small rally and indicated a decline of a similar duration. During that decline we see another pattern (B), followed by a 4-day rally and another engulfing pattern. Since this rally was relatively brief, so was the new trend signaled by the pattern (C)—1 day in fact. Then we see a dragonfly doji, a form of bullish hammer, and the price bottoms. Finally, another engulfing pattern (D) signals a decline lasting barely a day. In a very general sense, we can see from this and the previous chart that the power of a candlestick pattern often depends on the kind of trend it follows. In other words, a pattern that forms after a long uptrend—say, a couple of weeks—will have a tendency to be stronger than one which appears after a 2- or

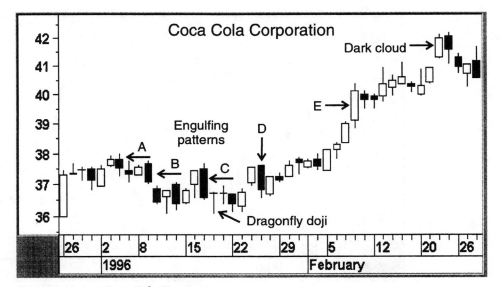

CHART 11-2. *Coca Cola Corporation.*

3-day price move. I say tendency because there are no guarantees in technical analysis.

As the rally progresses, you can see that a long white day
(E) is followed by 2 smaller black days. These are contained
within the trading range of the first, so when the third white
day closes at a new high we have a form of the rising-three
methods. In this case, there are two contratrend days, so it's
really a rising-two method.

Finally, we can see a dark cloud cover right at the peak of
the rally. See how the second day opens above the first and
then closes just a little bit below the midpoint of the white
real body.

Chart 11-3 shows a Chicago futures chart for the yen. One
thing you may notice is the substantial number of gaps early
on. They occur because a considerable amount of trading is
done outside the Chicago time zone. The same kind of phenomena occur with securities that are very illiquid. It is very
important to bear this in mind when interpreting candlestick
charts. What appears to be a gap may just be a distortion
resulting from time zone differences or just plain illiquidity in
the marketplace.

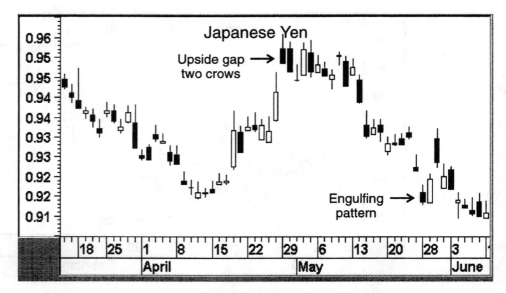

CHART 11-3. *Japanese yen.*

At any rate, Chart 11-3 shows a pattern which meets all the requirements of an upside gap with two crows. First, we have an uptrend culminating in a long white day. The next day sees an upward-gapping black day, followed by a second black day which opens above the first, then closes below it. Finally, the close of this engulfing day is still above the open of the long white day—that is, a gap is still present.

Chart 11-4 shows a shooting star, because the black upside-gapping day opens and closes close to the low, resulting in a small real body and a relatively long wick. Since the second black day still maintains the gap above the first day's opening, you may think of an upside gap with two crows. However, this pattern requires that the second black day engulf the first, which it clearly does not. In any event, the price declines, whatever the name of the pattern.

The bottom of the decline is signaled by a gravestone doji. This is normally a bearish pattern when it appears after an advance, but occasionally (as in this case) can be bullish after a decline.

The next top is signaled by an evening star. The qualifications are a long white candle (the color of the first day should

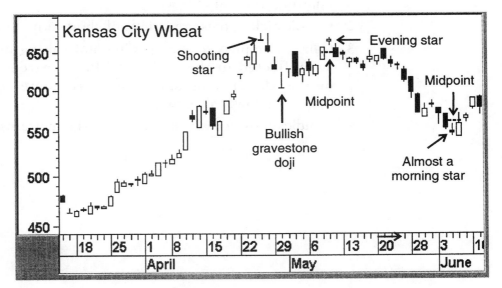

CHART 11-4. *Kansas City wheat.*

be in the direction of the trend), followed by a small real body that gaps up from the first day (the color is not material in this case), and finally a black candle that closes well below the first day's midpoint (indicated by the horizontal line).

The last formation that I have highlighted on this chart is what I call an "almost a morning star." This is because the pattern has most of the necessary attributes except one. The first day is a long black body which is in sympathy with the trend. The second is a small real body that gaps down. The third day is a long white candle, but it does not close above the midpoint of the first day, as indicated by the horizontal line.

This chapter has not explored the subject of candlesticks completely. However, a sufficient grounding has been provided to help you appreciate some of the finer points of this method and hopefully to whet your appetite for further study.

CANDLESTICK SUMMARY

1. Candlesticks display the same information as western bar charts but often in a way that alerts the trader to a trend reversal in a more timely manner than traditional western charting techniques.

2. Candlestick signals are strictly of short-term duration.

3. Candles emphasize the opening and closing prices which are reflected in the real body. Price extremes that fall beyond the opening and closing prices are portrayed by upper and lower shadows.

4. Candles form reversal and continuation patterns.

SOME QUICK TIPS ON PRACTICAL TRADING TACTICS

It's all very well knowing the principles and theory of technical analysis, but it is equally important to be able to put them into practice, and that's what this chapter is all about. The successful application of technical analysis requires sound money management practices. You must also be prepared to change your position if market conditions change or if things do not work out as you originally expected. In some respects, this chapter will review some of the more practical aspects that we have already covered. I'll try to answer two vital questions: where to buy and where to sell.

GOOD PLACES TO ENTER POSITIONS

One of the first tasks whenever you are considering entering a position is to assess your estimated risk relative to the potential reward. Generally, you should not enter a trade unless this ratio is at least 3 to 1. Since this is an estimate, you must be careful not to let the wish father the thought, and be realistic about the assumptions. Figure 12-1 shows a reverse head-and-shoulders formation. Suppose we decide to buy on the breakout. What is the potential reward? What is the risk? Well, the reward, as best we know it, is the price objective. This is the distance between the head and the neckline projected up. The risk, on the other hand, is the point where the price does not perform as expected—the level at which we would place our stop loss. In this case, a good benchmark is

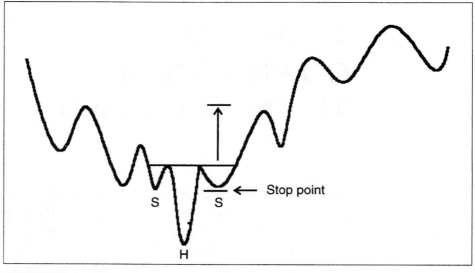

FIGURE 12-1.

just below the right shoulder. Here the risk, or stop point, is more than outweighed by the potential, as indicated by the minimum upside projection. The lower area of the right shoulder is important because it represents support. Also, a violation of the right shoulder would indicate that the series of rising bottoms that began with the head had been broken. The fact that the price not only pulled back into the body of the pattern but penetrated a key support area would be sufficient to liquidate the position.

The process of placing a stop, or at least mentally rehearsing where to get out, is vitally important. It sets you up psychologically for recognizing that things may, and probably will, go wrong. When the price declines, it is all too easy to hold on in the hope it will recover. Never rely on hope; rely on the facts as you see them. If you were sitting on the sidelines and saw the price slip below the right shoulder, you would probably never consider a purchase. If you buy the security on the basis of the breakout and the breakout fails, there is no reason to hold it any longer.

In our discussion of price patterns earlier, it became obvious that since a breakout represents a trend reversal signal, it is a good entry point. However, it may not always be convenient to buy in the excitement that often takes place during a breakout, since the price may move too fast. This is especially true in the highly leveraged futures markets, where a few seconds' delay can cost thousands of dollars. Chart 12-1 shows an alternate entry point. Since prices often retrace part of a move, it is a good idea to enter the market as the price moves back to the breakout level. Remember, support and resistance reverse their roles, so if the price level was formerly important resistance on the way up, it should now be equally important as a support zone on the way down. The problem most of us have is that we don't have the same kind of buying enthusiasm when prices are retreating as when they are advancing, yet these are usually better places to enter the market.

In Chart 12-2 the price breaks out from a reverse head-and-shoulders pattern. Again we see a nice retracement move as the price moves back to support in the area of the extended neckline.

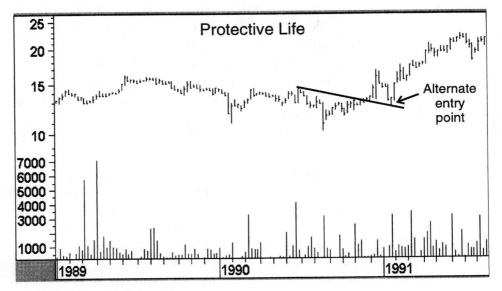

CHART 12-1. *Protective Life.*

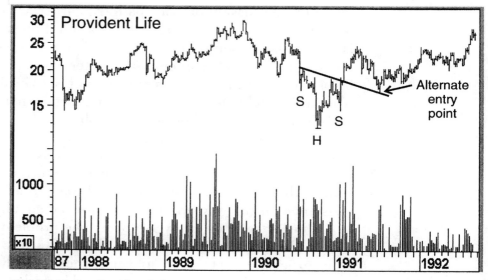

CHART 12-2. *Provident Life.*

The alternative is to buy once you get a signal that the retracement move has terminated and prices are once again advancing. In Figure 12-2 we see a nice breakout from a broadening formation with a flat top. The rally was probably too steep to buy into. However, a retracement move took the price back to the breakout point. Note how the volume shrank during this decline. This is a positive sign, since volume is going with the trend. Had the volume expanded during the retracement process, there would have been cause for concern. In this situation it was possible to construct a trendline joining the declining peaks. The violation of the trendline would then have provided a low-risk entry point. In this case, the stop would have been placed below the horizontal line representing the top of the broadening pattern. To place it below the low of this pattern would have been far too risky. As I mentioned, it is very important to keep an eye out for volume trends, since volume should contract as the retracement gets under way. It is surprising that the most emotional breakouts are often followed by retracement moves. Just as gaps can rep-

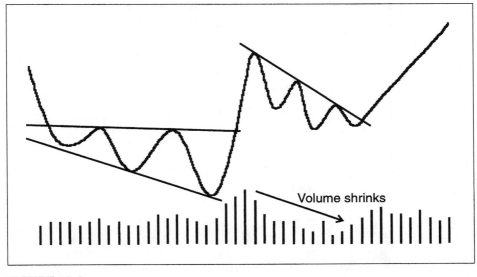

FIGURE 12-2.

resent highly emotional moves and are usually closed, so emotional breakouts may suffer the same fate. In sum, volume should expand on the breakout, contract on the retracement, and then expand again as the retracement move reverses.

Chart 12-3 shows another low-risk buying opportunity. It develops after a good down trendline has been violated on the upside and the price retreats back to the extended line. Again, we are looking at the reversal in the line's role as one of resistance to one of support. Generally speaking, the more significant the trendline prior to its violation, the stronger its role as a support zone. There are two possible entry points. The first occurs when the line is touched. The second arises when the short-term decline reverses direction (alternate entry point). Of course, the market may not oblige by offering either of these possibilities. That is why it is important to continually monitor your database for suitable candidates.

The same principle of retracement can be applied to moving averages. Chart 12-4 uses the same data for Russ Berrie that we looked at before, but this time a 65-week EMA has

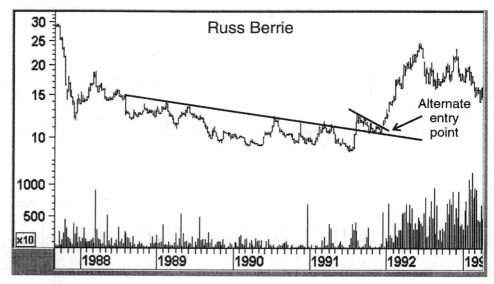

CHART 12-3. *Russ Berrie.*

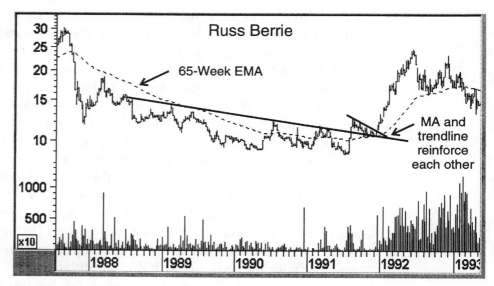

CHART 12-4. *Russ Berrie.*

been plotted. You can see how the price fell right back to it in the same area as the extended trendline. In this instance, the average and the line definitely reinforce each other as support.

Chart 12-5, showing the price of Safeco, is in a bull market. In 1991 and 1993 it retreats back to the 65-week EMA (the dashed line). These are good entry points in themselves. However, you can also see that the 13-week rate of change, plotted in the lower panel, is also at the minus-10 oversold level. This tells us that the price not only has reached support (the EMA), but is also oversold. Again we have two good entry points, as marked by the arrows. The stops could have been placed a safe distance under the EMA. You may have noticed that the overbought line is not very sensibly constructed, because it includes too many rallies. I realize this, but the idea here is that we are trying to establish realistic oversold levels in a bull market. Had I used a more realistic plus 15 percent and corresponding 15 percent for the oversolds, there would have been no oversold readings at all during this 3-year period.

Sometimes a good low-risk entry point occurs after the price is oversold and you can spot an outside day from a bar

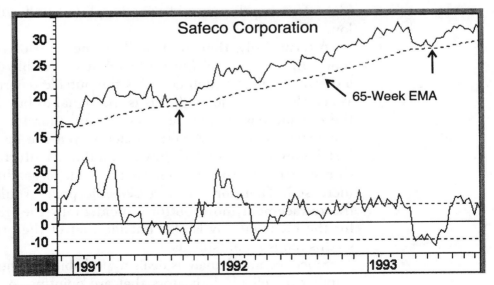

CHART 12-5. *Safeco Corporation.*

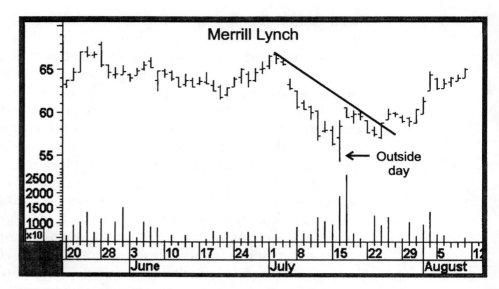

CHART 12-6.   *Merrill Lynch.*

chart. Chart 12-6 is a one-day reversal signal and indicates a form of emotional climax. It is possible to go long during the outside day itself, as the price rallies above the previous day's high. The stop loss would then be placed under the intraday low.

Alternatively, there is usually some kind of retracement move. In this chart of Merrill Lynch it is possible to construct a down trendline which contains the outside-day retracement. When the line is violated, this is the signal to buy. The low on the outside day is quite a ways off and therefore provides a somewhat large risk. A better place to put the stop would be just below the extended down trendline. Unfortunately the line continues to decline, so the risk is gradually being increased. Therefore, a more sensible point would be below the retracement move bottom. Incidentally the trading range for the breakout day is also outside that of the previous one, so this too is an outside day!

Since technical analysis deals in probabilities, the greater the number of reliable indicators that are pointing in a particular direction the more reliable the signal is likely to be. In Chart 12-7 we see substantial evidence that the trend has reversed. The dashed line is a 30-day simple moving average. On two occasions the price is able to violate both the average and the trendline, and each time a worthwhile rally follows. The two have a habit of reinforcing each other so the signal is generally more reliable than if the price had penetrated just one of them. If you think of both the trendline and the moving average as being dynamic areas of resistance, you can appreciate that a joint penetration of the two of them is like penetrating a very formidable level of resistance.

Moreover, if this kind of situation can be reinforced with a trendline break or other reversal signal in a momentum indicator as in Chart 12-8, the evidence is even more overwhelming. This happens to be a 25-day rate-of-change. During the January breakout it was not possible to draw a trendline, but it certainly was possible on the May rally. Notice also, how the volume expanded at this time. Consequently we had numerous pieces of evidence that the trend had reversed.

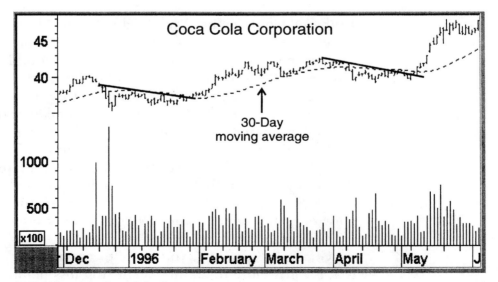

CHART 12-7. *Coca Cola Corporation.*

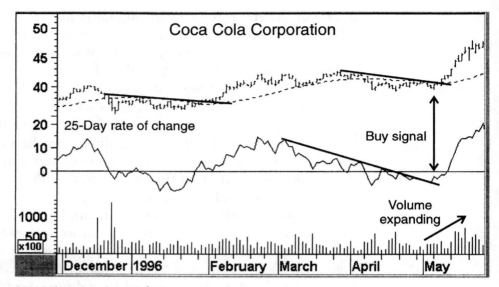

CHART 12-8. *Coca Cola Corporation.*

GOOD PLACES TO TAKE PROFITS OR CUT LOSSES

In the previous section I touched on a few ideas about where to set stop loss points. Now it is time to consider some more. It is usually pretty easy to get into a position. The problem most of us have is getting out, either by taking profits or by cutting losses. That's why it is mandatory when entering a trade to have some idea of where you will take profits if things go your way; and more importantly, where you should limit your losses if things do not go according to plan. If you talk to most successful traders you will find that they tend to look down before they look up, by which I mean that they are always looking over their shoulder by anticipating what could go wrong and mentally rehearsing an exit strategy that either limits losses or protects profits.

Generally speaking, you want to enter a trade at a price that is fairly close to an intelligent stop loss point. In that way the risk factor will be significantly reduced. The question you should ask yourself when placing a stop is "Where does the price have to go in order to considerably lower the odds that the prevailing trend is up?" Since these are trading, as opposed to investment, decisions the prevailing trend in this case will either be short or intermediate in nature. Generally speaking, you need to keep an eye out for critical support points. When a support level has been penetrated the odds that a trend reversal has taken place are increased. These could be actual levels, a trendline, an extended trendline, a moving average or a previous minor low.

In Figure 12-3 we have the best of all worlds since the price triggers a sell signal when it crosses the moving average, marked by the dashed line, the solid trendline and the previous minor low.

Another question is whether a stop should be placed on an intraday or close-only basis (Chart 12-9). Let's suppose you were short during this decline in the Platinum price, where should you cover on a break of a close-only or line chart, or on a break of a bar chart? Since a close-only chart reflects the positions traders are willing to take home overnight, they are

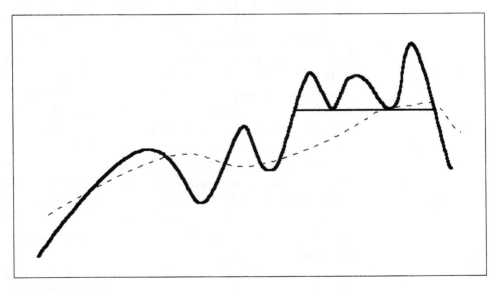

FIGURE 12-3.

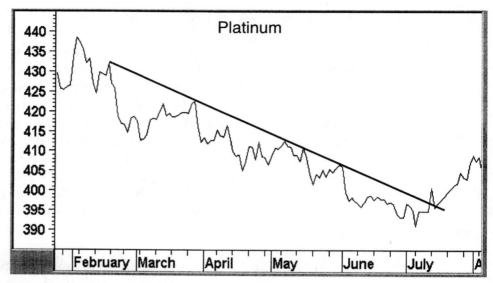

CHART 12-9. *Platinum.*

usually more reliable. In this chart the solid line joins the closes. It's a pretty good one because it has been touched or approached on several occasions. Now, if we look at Chart 12-10, I've constructed a trendline that touches the intraday highs. That's the dashed one. The solid line is also a good one, but it is quite obvious that it is violated later than the close-only line. Normally, trendlines on bar charts are violated first. This just happens to be an exception which indicates that common sense and flexibility is preferable to hard and fast rules set in stone. Another reason why bar charts may not be as reliable is that the price may violate the line during the trading session and then rally back above it by the close. Bar charts therefore are relatively more subject to whipsaws. Don't forget that intraday sessions are subject to manipulation and rumor, far more than closing prices when traders have to decide whether they are going to take a position home overnight.

Chart 12-11 of London Copper is a little trickier since the trendline is declining and so the theoretical downside limit is

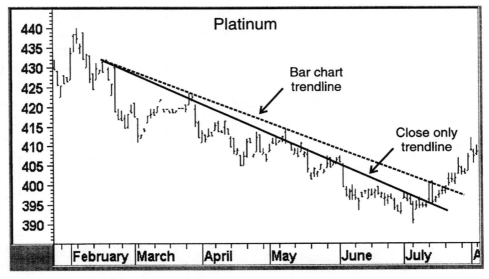

CHART 12-10. *Platinum.*

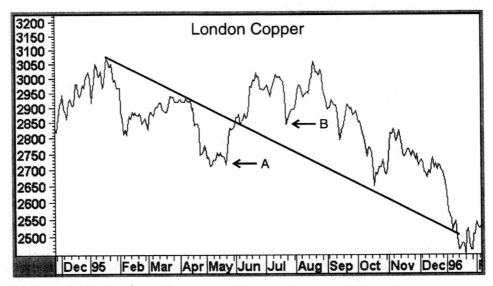

CHART 12-11. *London copper.*

zero. The safest thing to do is to establish an actual level of support below which you are unwilling to take the position at the outset. Generally, this should be a previous minor bottom such as point A in this chart. This may be a bit too much to risk, so if a subsequent, and higher, minor low, such as the one at point B develops, that would be the preferred choice. As you can see, if the stop had been placed below the trend-line it would gradually have been paced lower and lower down to unacceptable levels. It is also worth noting that if a trend-line is going to act as good support, the price will typically use it as a springboard, quickly bouncing off it rather than hugging close to it for several days.

In Chart 12-12, the entry point for the trade at point A is a pretty good one. The stop would normally be placed at the previous minor low at point B. However, as the price rises so the risk is increased. It therefore makes sense to try to find a higher stop point. One possibility is to find and then use a reliable moving average. Another, is to study the price action and wait for a minor low to develop, and use it. Finally, in this particular case it was possible to construct a trendline joining

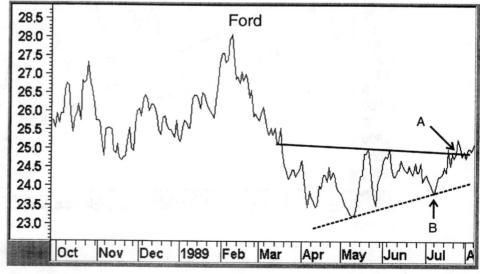

CHART 12-12. *Ford.*

the two lows as shown in Chart 12-13. As it turned out, the price did form a minor low at point X, and this proved to be more timely than waiting for the trendline violation. Had we chosen to be more aggressive in placing a stop, as illustrated in Chart 12-14, it would have been possible to recognize a small upward sloping head and shoulders distribution pattern right at the top of the rally. However, since the base from which the breakout had originally taken place was quite large, it was reasonable to expect that the rally would have been more substantial than actually turned out. An alternative policy would have been to take partial profits when the head and shoulders was completed. Or even when the relatively steep trendline joining the July and August lows was violated.

One important thing to bear in mind is that flat, or gently rising or falling moving average crossovers (Chart 12-15) tend to be more reliable than penetrations where the average has a sharp angle of ascent or descent. This means that in a sharply rising trend a retracement into the area of the moving average is more likely to find support. In effect, a reaction to a moving average with a sharp angle of ascent is likely to provide a low risk buying point. The average itself can then be used as a stop

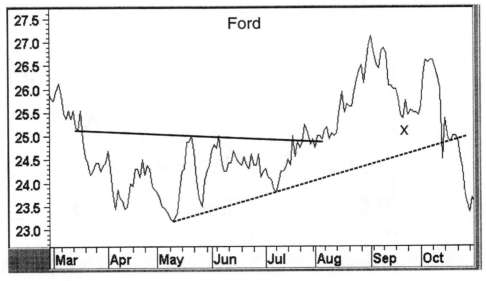

CHART 12-13. *Ford.*

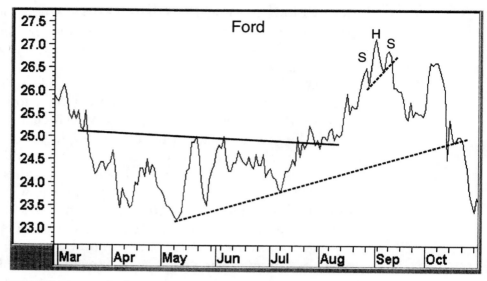

CHART 12-14. *Ford.*

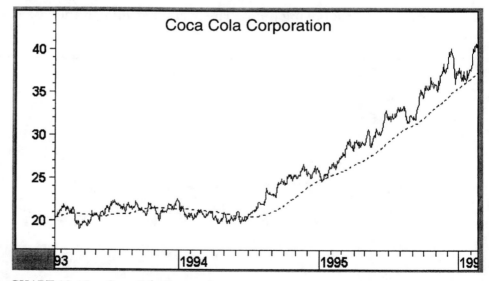

CHART 12-15. *Coca Cola Corporation.*

loss point. Or, I should say, the area underneath the moving average. Also, since the average is rising at a fairly fast rate, it is easy to keep raising the stop, thereby protecting larger and larger amounts of profit.

Chart 12-15, of Coca Cola Corporation, features a 100-day simple moving average. During the trading range action of 1994 it was a very misleading indicator. However, as the bull market got underway, reactions back to the average proved to be excellent intermediate entry points.

Chart 12-16 shows a more fortunate situation in which profits are taken, rather than losses being cut. The idea is that when a momentum indicator reaches an overbought reading following a good breakout, this is an intelligent place for taking at least partial profits. Of course this is not a trend reversal signal, but it does represent a point where the price is likely to run into some profit taking in the form of a peak of at least temporary proportion.

In Chart 12-17, we see an outside day in Newmont Mining following a rally. Since an outside day represents a temporary peak in investor emotion it is also a good place to at least take

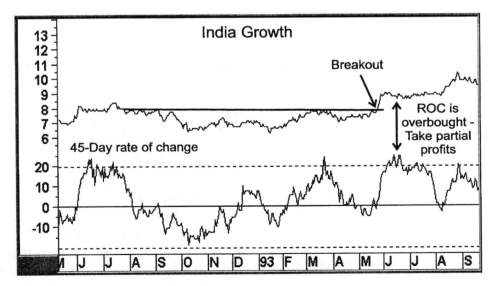

CHART 12-16. *India Growth Fund.*

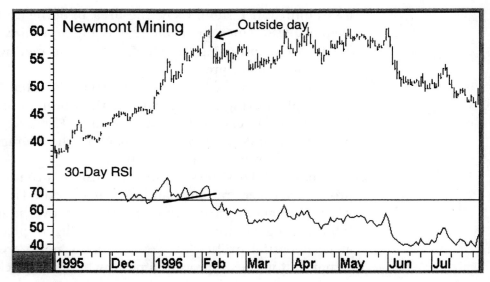

CHART 12-17.   *Newmont Mining.*

partial profits. In this case it was supported by the fact that the 30-Day RSI not only completed a top, but also broke below its overbought zone on its way back towards a neutral reading.

HOW TO DEAL WITH FALSE BREAKOUTS

Unfortunately false breakouts are a fact of life. Even when we get a decisive breakout from a price pattern on exceptional volume, such as the one shown in Chart 12-18, you may still be exposed to a whipsaw. The first thing to do before entering a trade is to decide where you will get out if things go wrong. This is especially important when the breakout looks convincing, because then you will be in a very complacent frame of mind, believing that there is no way that the breakout is a whipsaw. We saw earlier that the place to put a stop for an inverse head and shoulders failure is just below the low of the right shoulder (line A).

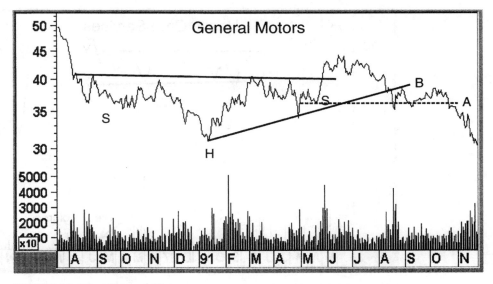

CHART 12-18. *General Motors.*

An alternative is to construct a line joining the head and the low of the right shoulder (line B). This is not always so reliable, but certainly gives an earlier warning.

Rectangles are quite difficult (Chart 12-19) if you are not prepared to hold the position until the lower level of the rectangle is breached at point X. One solution is to place a stop under the upper boundary of the pattern, working on the assumption that if the breakout does not hold, then the odds of it being a valid one are greatly reduced. An alternative would be to place the stop under the previous minor low, if there is one, as in this example. An even better way is to look at the volume pattern on the breakout before you buy. In this case it didn't amount to much, so there was already an early warning sign that the breakout would prove disappointing.

In Chart 12-20 we see another way in which a false breakout may be anticipated. See how the 14-day RSI was in overbought territory as the price was breaking out.

This chart of silver futures (Chart 12-21) offers another warning since the breakout developed on an intraday basis. By

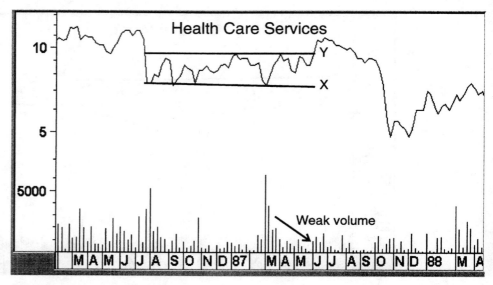

CHART 12-19. *Health Care Services.*

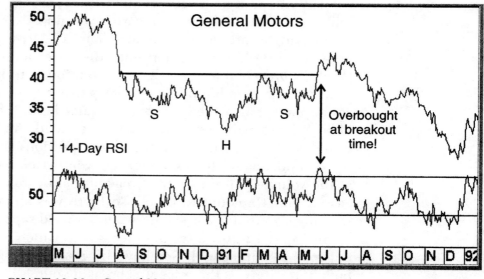

CHART 12-20. *General Motors.*

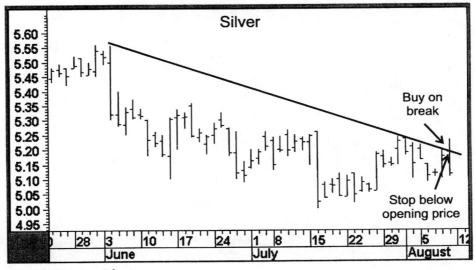

CHART 12-21.   *Silver.*

the time of the close the price had retreated well back into the pattern. A good approach, if you had bought on the breakout, would have been to have liquidated when the price broke back below the session opening. Opening prices, as we learned from the chapter on candlesticks, is a fairly important emotional point on the chart.

SUMMARY

1. If an upside breakout is particularly strong, a better place to make purchases is on the retracement.

2. Always mentally rehearse where you are going to bail out in case the markets go against you. Mentally or physically place a stop loss before you enter a trade.

3. When placing stops, look for good support areas. These can be actual levels, previous minor lows, trendlines, or moving averages.

4. Avoid low-volume and overbought upside breakouts.

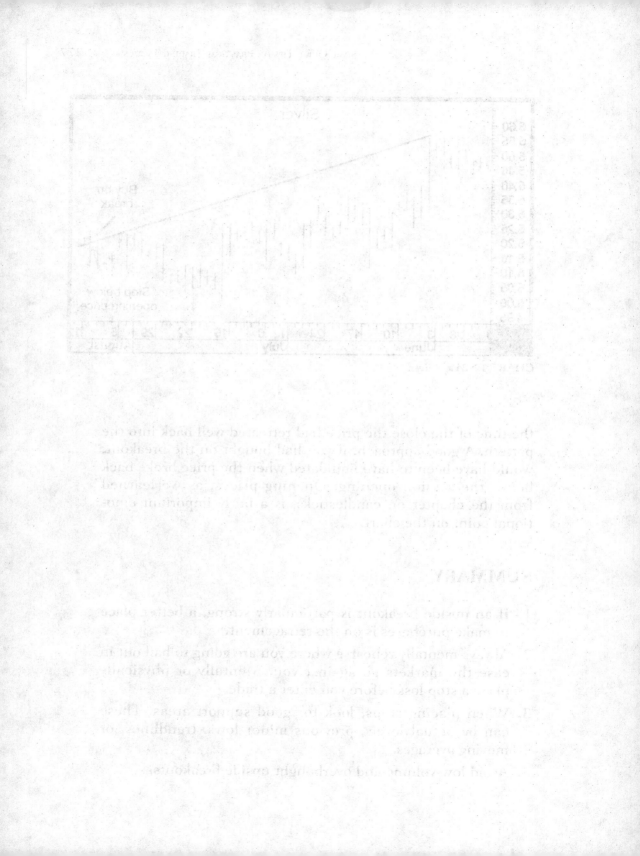

APPENDIX

To Install the *Introduction to Technical Analysis* CD

1. Place the CD in your computer's CD player text side up. *The CD must be in the CD player whenever you use this program.* During the installation process, several files (a total of 8 to 11 MB) will be copied to your computer's hard drive to control the CD's operation. It does not put the entire tutorial on the hard drive.

2. Go to the Start button in the lower left corner of your Windows screen, select Run and type **D:\setup.exe** in the text box, then click **OK**. If your CD player is a different drive than D, replace the D with the correct drive; i.e., **X:\setup.exe**.

3. On the first screen, "Select an option"—choose **Full—Install all files**. We recommend you do not change the destination directory that is **C:\Pring**, although you have the option, it keeps things simple when troubleshooting.

4. Please be patient while the files are transferred. The screen will show you the percentage of completion and prompt you when it's done.

5. After the files are copied, you are prompted: Do you want setup to create Program Manager groups? Select **Yes**. This creates a **Pring** folder for this tutorial and any other Martin Pring tutorials you may

install in the future, making it easy to locate them in the program directory. (Older tutorials may be found in the IIER directory.)

6. The Program Group called Pring will appear; this is part of the installation process, so *do not try to start the program at this time*. Wait for the next screen to appear which will inform you that Installation is complete. Click **OK** and close the dialog by clicking on the "X" in the upper right-hand corner.

7. To run the tutorial, *be sure the CD is in your CD player* with the text side up, click on **Start**, then **Programs**, then on **Pring** and select the tutorial in the flyout menu.

8. The IIER logo will appear along with a loading message. During this time, the program is running a diagnostics to make sure you have the proper hardware to run the CD.

   PLEASE BE PATIENT! This is a large program and will only run as fast as your computer will run. Please don't click buttons or press the Esc key, as you may lock up your system and have to reboot. You will know that you're on your way when the music begins.

9. When you reach the Welcome Page, please take the time to watch *How to Play the Movies*. This will explain how to maneuver through the tutorial and explain certain important features.

FOR CDs THAT OFFER INTERNET ACCESS:

10. If you are interested in other products the IIER offers, click on the Visit Our Web Site button. NOTE: You must be connected to your browser for this to work. You will be prompted to verify your browser. If this information is correct, then click **OK**.

TECHNICAL SUPPORT

To access the technical support guide located on the CD-ROM:

1. Right-click on the Start button and left-click on Explore.

2. Locate your CD-ROM drive and double-click on the file called **Support**.

3. This file can be viewed in WordPad or Word 97 (or higher). If you cannot access either of the files, please visit our site and access the file using the Adobe Acrobat Reader®.

For additional support issues and updates, please visit our web site at http://www.pring.com.

INDEX

ABOUT THE AUTHOR

When Martin Pring talks, investors listen. His book *Technical Analysis Explained* is considered the standard work in the field. Described in *Barron's* as a technician's technician, Martin J. Pring has lectured throughout the world on financial subjects and is the editor of two monthly publications: the *Intermarket Review* and the *Global Chart Book*. He is a prolific author and has produced numerous video and CD-ROM products for investors. Martin has been featured in *Barron's*, the *International Herald Tribune, Futures Magazine, Technical Analysis of Stocks & Commodities,* and other leading publications serving the financial community.

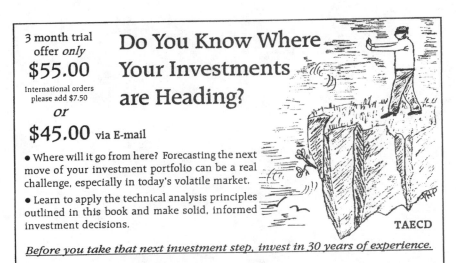

SOFTWARE AND INFORMATION LICENSE

The software and information on this diskette (collectively referred to as the "Product") are the property of The McGraw-Hill Companies, Inc. ("McGraw-Hill") and are protected by both United States copyright law and international copyright treaty provision. You must treat this Product just like a book, except that you may copy it into a computer to be used and you may make archival copies of the Products for the sole purpose of backing up our software and protecting your investment from loss.

By saying "just like a book," McGraw-Hill means, for example, that the Product may be used by any number of people and may be freely moved from one computer location to another, so long as there is no possibility of the Product (or any part of the Product) being used at one location or on one computer while it is being used at another. Just as a book cannot be read by two different people in two different places at the same time, neither can the Product be used by two different people in two different places at the same time (unless, of course, McGraw-Hill's rights are being violated).

McGraw-Hill reserves the right to alter or modify the contents of the Product at any time.

This agreement is effective until terminated. The Agreement will terminate automatically without notice if you fail to comply with any provisions of this Agreement. In the event of termination by reason of your breach, you will destroy or erase all copies of the Product installed on any computer system or made for backup purposes and shall expunge the Product from your data storage facilities.

LIMITED WARRANTY

McGraw-Hill warrants the physical diskette(s) enclosed herein to be free of defects in materials and workmanship for a period of sixty days from the purchase date. If McGraw-Hill receives written notification within the warranty period of defects in materials or workmanship, and such notification is determined by McGraw-Hill to be correct, McGraw-Hill will replace the defective diskette(s). Send request to:

Customer Service
McGraw-Hill
Gahanna Industrial Park
860 Taylor Station Road
Blacklick, OH 43004-9615

The entire and exclusive liability and remedy for breach of this Limited Warranty shall be limited to replacement of defective diskette(s) and shall not include or extend to any claim for or right to cover any other damages, including but not limited to, loss of profit, data, or use of the software, or special, incidental, or consequential damages or other similar claims, even if McGraw-Hill has been specifically advised as to the possibility of such damages. In no event will McGraw-Hill's liability for any damages to you or any other person ever exceed the lower of suggested list price or actual price paid for the license to use the Product, regardless of any form of the claim.

THE McGRAW-HILL COMPANIES, INC. SPECIFICALLY DISCLAIMS ALL OTHER WARRANTIES, EXPRESS OR IMPLIED, INCLUDING BUT NOT LIMITED TO, ANY IMPLIED WARRANTY OF MERCHANTABILITY OR FITNESS FOR A PARTICULAR PURPOSE. Specifically, McGraw-Hill makes no representation or warranty that the Product is fit for any particular purpose and any implied warranty of merchantability is limited to the sixty day duration of the Limited Warranty covering the physical diskette(s) only (and not the software or in-formation) and is otherwise expressly and specifically disclaimed.

This Limited Warranty gives you specific legal rights; you may have others which may vary from state to state. Some states do not allow the exclusion of incidental or consequential damages, or the limitation on how long an implied warranty lasts, so some of the above may not apply to you.

This Agreement constitutes the entire agreement between the parties relating to use of the Product. The terms of any purchase order shall have no effect on the terms of this Agreement. Failure of McGraw-Hill to insist at any time on strict compliance with this Agreement shall not constitute a waiver of any rights under this Agreement. This Agreement shall be construed and governed in accordance with the laws of New York. If any provision of this Agreement is held to be contrary to law, that provision will be enforced to the maximum extent permissible and the remaining provisions will remain in force and effect.